Len Arbery

THE COMPLETE BOOK OF RIVER FISHING

David & Charles

● (Page 1) *The author's first ever 5lb+ chub, from the Kennet;* (page 2) *Peter Frost fishes a windswept Dorset Stour*

This book is dedicated to the fond memory of my very dear friend and fellow Herts-Chiltern Anglers member, Alec Lewis, who never uttered an unkind word about anybody.

> *God grant that I may live to fish*
> *Until my dying day;*
> *And when it comes to my last cast*
> *I then most humbly pray,*
> *When in the Lord's safe landing-net*
> *I'm peacefully asleep,*
> *That in His mercy I be judged*
> *As good enough to keep.*

(H. Burman)

164 7 104566 12016

Illustrations by Yvonne Kavanagh

A DAVID & CHARLES BOOK

Copyright © Len Arbery 1993

First published 1993

Len Arbery has asserted his right to be identified as author of this work in accordance with the Copyright, Designs and Patents Act 1988.

A catalogue record for this book is available from the British Library.

ISBN 0 7153 9928 4

Typeset by Ace Filmsetting Ltd, Frome
and printed in Great Britian by Redwood Press Ltd
for David & Charles
Brunel House Newton Abbot Devon

THE COMPLETE BOOK OF
RIVER FISHING

Foreword

Many books have been written about river fishing, but this one is different. Instead of a list of chapters on the different species, Len Arbery writes only about those that he has long experience and knowledge of.

But this is not a book just about catching big fish; there is much more to it than that. Emphasis is given to location, and rightly so for, as the late Dick Walker so often said, you cannot catch a fish that isn't there. For instance, on chub he says that 'Raft swims rarely produce very big chub . . . anything that deters other anglers is always worth investigating . . . a swim with an even steady flow is more likely to produce than a rough or boiling one.'

Len stresses the importance of good tackle and how tackle affects presentation. Drennan's Star Point hooks, for instance, because of their lightness against an eyed hook 'improves bait presentation'. Such attention to detail – and this is only one instance amidst many – puts big fish on the bank that may not have otherwise picked up the bait or rejected it. On chub, the author's advice to fish difficult swims is also sound: 'It seems some chub anglers are too worried about getting hung up . . . passing up the chance of a specimen chub in the process.'

When I was still in short trousers, an experienced angler pointed out a chub swim to me. 'But,' I said, 'it's very weedy; if I hooked one I wouldn't land it.' 'Peter,' my tutor said, 'hook the fish first, then start worrying.' Fifty years on I have never forgotten that advice.

This book leans toward barbel, the author's favourite river species and, riverwise, the 'in' fish. Len writes of barbel leaping clear of the water, a fact which is never mentioned by other present-day writers, although I have witnessed it many times. Many writers believe that barbel only give 'big' bites, but Len lays great emphasis on the small, often insignificant, twitches and pulls that the barbel fisher can expect.

Fishing beach-caster style in fast water; flavouring loaves; how to beat floating weed when legering; placing a cube of polystyrene on the hook when stalking barbel and the discovery that big individual fish in a shoal have their own 'feeding lines' is all up-to-date information.

This book is not written by one of the sport's 'instant experts' but by someone of long experience. But Len does more than simply fish: he studies the habits and feeding patterns of his chosen quarry and is not afraid to read and digest what some of the great masters of the past – Martin, Coxon, Sheringham, Walker, etc – wrote. Their observations coincide with Len's own experiences.

With many fine and outstanding river fish – chub to 6lb 9oz and a near-record barbel (14lb exactly) to his credit – Len is well qualified to write of his experiences. My criteria of a good book is that if I glean just one snippet of information which will put fish on my hook, it has been well worth the cover price. When I finally put this book down, I had gleaned not just one snippet, but several. Few, if any, anglers will read this book without adding to their knowledge; most will glean a great deal. Those who read and digest this informative, thought-provoking book cannot fail to become better anglers for it.

PETER STONE
Oxford, 1992

Contents

Introduction

River fishing is ignored by a large proportion of anglers, which is perhaps understandable: some of our freshwater fish do not grow as big in rivers as they do in stillwaters. Furthermore, learning to appreciate and cope with the problems involved and associated with running water takes much time and effort and involves a certain amount of hard work. With the present hectic pace of life, many anglers have no wish to go to such lengths. All I can say to such people is that they are missing much and I hope that this book will provide an insight and some short-cuts to the delights of the riverbank. My own angling career has been spent in the pursuit of big fish in both still and running water, and I would not have missed either for anything.

Since time immemorial great river catches have excited, influenced and fired anglers' imaginations. And, even though they are well documented, some of these feats still provide almost incredible reading. Writing in 1896, the old 'Trent Otter' (John William Martin), in his book *Barbel and Chub Fishing*, tells this story:

One of the very best bags of barbel that I have authentic information about was captured by poor Owen, a former Newark tackle maker. Many years have passed since he was laid to his last rest. I remember the old chap and his funny little shop, hung round with curious old fishing prints. These memories stir up feelings that only anglers can appreciate. He pointed out to me with no little pride a page in his fishing journal, and let me copy it. It was a short account of the very best day's barbel fishing he ever enjoyed on the Trent. I find on reference that nearly fifty years have passed and gone since that, for him, eventful day. His bag had in it 32 barbel, five of which weighed from 12 to 15lbs, each; about a dozen more ranged from 6 to 10lbs each, and the remainder were between 3 and 6lbs each, the whole lot going no less than 224lbs, being an average of 7lbs per fish – a most extraordinary

bag.... I may have seen one or two lots of barbel that exceeded Owen's in number, but I certainly never did see a bag that contained anything like such large fish.

More recently, the Royalty Fishery on the Hampshire Avon has provided some staggering catches, although it is true that many successful anglers fishing there in the early days had graduated from the great academy of river angling that once existed on the River Trent. J. W. Martin had met and learned from the likes of Thomas Sunman, Charlie Hudson, Thomas Bentley, Frank Sims, George Holland ('Nottingham George'), and, perhaps most importantly, William Bailey, author of *The Angler's Instructor*, in 1857. Martin, in turn, aided Henry Coxon's development as a master angler. Coxon is renowned as the inventor of the most successful centre-pin reel ever – the Aerial – thus his name will live in perpetuity. Due to the Trent's sad decline, Coxon and his Nottingham angling partner, F. W. K. Wallis, found it necessary to travel south, to the banks of the Royalty Fishery, to continue their search for specimen river fish. And the fabulous fishing they enjoyed may be imagined by the following.

During September 1933 Wallis caught over 60 Royalty barbel, including specimens of 14lb 4oz, 13lb 8oz, 5 over 11lb and 3 over 10lb (all of which were returned to the water). In two days' fishing in 1937, Wallis shared with Claude Taylor a catch of 17 barbel all over 9lb, and there were 5 fish over 12lb, the best a record equalling fish of 14lb 6oz coming to Wallis' rod.

After World War II, the name Bill Warren was synonymous with mind-blowing catches, most, but by no means all, from the Royalty. For example, from the Bull Water at Downton, on 8 December 1945, Capt Len Parker reported the 'best show I have seen in over 40 years' angling'. Bill and his brother Sonny caught no less than 72 roach that day, 17 of which were 2lb and over. Nine of these roach were set up by J. Cooper & Son

in the same glass case. On the same day they had 4 chub between 3lb 8oz and 4lb 8oz as well.

But it is Bill Warren's barbel and chub catches that are phenomenal. In one four-month period in the winter of 1961–2 he caught 21 double-figure barbel, the three heaviest weighed 12lb 8oz, 12lb 10oz and 13lb 4oz. In the 1953–4 season, Bill caught no less than 306 chub, 18 of which were over 5lb; all told, he caught 234 chub of 5lb or over, 25 over 6lb, plus chub of 7lb 3oz and 7lb 6oz.

It is said that a member of the Piscatorial Society, E. J. Walker, was the first angler to discover the large chub in the Royalty. Fittingly, Walker took advantage of his knowledge in the shape of two 7-pounders – 7lb exactly and 7lb 5oz. Mr F. W. Smith's 1906 Royalty-caught 7lb 6½oz chub headed the record list until December 1913, when G. F. Smith's 8lb 4oz monster, also from the Royalty, was taken.

Notwithstanding its obvious domination, not all the Hampshire Avon's 7lb-plus chub have come from the

● *Bill Warren's guest-house was a rendezvous for notable anglers.* Left to right: *Ken Taylor, Brian Cotterell, A. N. Other, Bill Warren, Peter Stone, Joe Taylor, Peter Drennan, and Fred J. Taylor with his hand to his head. The mirror and the fish on the wall were part of the catch made by Bill and Sonny Warren, which Capt L. A. Parker said was 'The best show I've seen in over 40 years' angling.'* (Peter Stone)

Royalty. From further upstream have come Dr Lewis-Smith's ('Silver Doctor') 7lb 6oz and Roger Newman's 7lb 8oz specimens; the story behind the latter fish, the biggest fully authentic chub of recent years, is included in Chapter 10.

Despite the twin evils of pollution and abstraction, rivers continue to produce exceptional catches. In the winter of 1989–90, while being filmed by Hugh Miles for the BBC2 television series, *A Passion for Angling*, Bob James captured a most remarkable bag of big roach. Bob lost count of exactly how many fish were caught; however, ten were in excess of 2lb 8oz and the heaviest two scaled 2lb 14oz and 2lb 15oz – one of the most impressive catches I have ever heard of. In addition to Bob James, *A Passion for Angling* also stars Chris Yates.

Further recent notable river catches include Martin Hooper's brace of 3lb roach; Ray Clarke's new 'record' roach, described in Chapter 10; and Pete Reading's grayling catches, topped by that magnificent 3lb 8oz specimen. Dave Howes, who has caught no less than eleven roach of 3lb and over, topped by a 3lb 8oz 8dm specimen, should not be forgotten.

Notwithstanding the foregoing, I realise, of course,

that success within angling, as with most other matters, means different things to different people. Yet the main purpose of this book is to try to help the angler who has already made the transition from the novice stage, no matter what his age, who wants not only to succeed with river fish, but who has the desire to catch much bigger fish than the norm. It is assumed that the reader will at least have a rudimentary knowledge of angling, so some everyday angling terms are not explained. Such explanations would unnecessarily increase the bulk of this work.

I make no apology for the large amount of space devoted to barbel. First, it is my firm belief that the majority of river anglers who want to catch big, hard-fighting fish, are more interested in barbel than in other species. Secondly, much of the information given for barbel is also relevant for other species. Pound for pound, the barbel probably fights more tenaciously than any other coarse fish in our rivers, a fact that has long been recognised: the poet, Michael Drayton, wrote

● *Bill Warren's 7lb 6oz ex-record chub, caught from the Royalty on 3 January 1957*

some four hundred years ago that 'The barbel, than which fish a braver doth not swim.' And that great angler and writer, the 'Trent Otter' (J. W. Martin), said of barbel at the beginning of this century, 'For bravery, he is a gem of the first water, and will fight it out to the very last gasp. He is very active, powerful, and vigorous, and is just the chap to try the angler's skill, and the strength of his tackle.' Consequently, the hunt for barbel demands both sound tackle and sound technique. Therefore, the successful barbel angler cannot help but become more successful with other species when he turns his mind in their direction. It is not surprising, therefore, that the barbel ranks second only to the mighty carp in the popularity stakes with Britain's big-fish anglers.

In his classic fishing book, *Still Water Angling*, Dick Walker laid down five basic essentials for catching big fish. As these 'essentials' are just as relevant for fish that live in moving water, it is important that we remind ourselves of them:

1 Locate the fish.
2 Don't frighten the fish.
3 Use the right tackle.
4 Fish at the right time.
5 Use the right bait.

Dick explained:

These are the five essentials, from what one might call a material point of view. I know that they do not cover the problem completely; what I want to stress is the importance of feeling your way to success, step by logical step. If you fish in this way, you are bound to succeed sooner or later.

● *Pete Reading's magnificent 3lb 8oz grayling* (Pete Reading)

● *2lb 15oz Windrush roach for the 'old master', Peter Stone (Peter Stone)*

These are very wise words indeed and they will be enlarged upon at the appropriate places.

Chapter 2 will cover what is considered to be the most important species. Some are important in their own right, while others are important for different reasons – such as their use as baits for predatory fish. There will not, therefore, be a complete list of all the river species, only those considered necessary to this work.

If the hints, tactics, wrinkles and tips contained herein – the result of more than a quarter of a century spent hunting big fish – help you to put some big fish on the bank, my main purpose has been achieved. However, it is hoped that this book shows my respect and high regard for my family and for my friends. I may not have caught as many big fish as other anglers, but I have certainly been blessed with the best of friends, who are more important to me than any fish, no matter how big that fish may be. My best friend is my wife: she puts up with all manner of comings and goings both by night and by day, and she is so tolerant and understanding of the reasons for leaving her alone when I have been at the waterside. Others who have enriched my life include Bob Buteux, Bill Quinlan, Kevin Clifford, Ron Chant and the late Alec Lewis, to whom this book is respectfully dedicated; my son Tony; Pete Cranstoun; Ritchie McDonald; Bob James and Bob Baker. In

Introduction

addition, there are those who have helped to make my river fishing so memorable: Richard Graham; Stef Horak; Pete Reading; Bob Moulsey; Chris Yates; Trefor West; Steve Harper; Tony Miles; Alan Brown; Martin Hooper; Pete Young; Dave Tissington; Bob Harrington; Newall White; Stuart Bruce; Keith Griffin; Edward Barder; Dave Ball; John Bailey; Ray Clarke; Alf Tapley; Peter Stone; John Wilson; Pete Frost; Pete Springate; Roger Newman; Dave Plowman; Dave Swallow; Jim Soden; Mick Newland; Alan Slater; Dave Steuart; Peter Drennan and last, but by no means least, living angling legend and great friend, 'Old Uncle Fred' – Fred J. Taylor. To these and to all those who have made fishing, for me at least, the most absorbing and enjoyable of leisure pursuits, I extend my heart-felt thanks.

Special thanks are due to Adrian Curtis, ex-News Editor of *Angling Times*. Because he is an extremely busy journalist, Adrian is unable to finish writing his own book. Nevertheless, when asked, he did not hesitate to make the time in his busy schedule to check my manuscript – an unselfish gesture for which I am extremely grateful.

I would also like to extend my thanks to the following for their valuable assistance and expertise in the preparation of this book. To Colin Dyson, one of the most respected voices in angling and once editor of *Coarse Angler*, not only for allowing extracts from that magazine, but also for the help and encouragement he gave me when my first fishing articles were penned. To Simon Roff, who has done so much to revive the fortunes of *Coarse Fisherman*, and who has also given me permission to quote from previously published articles of mine that appeared in his journal. To Neil Pope and Kevin Wilmot of that most important magazine, *Improve your Coarse Fishing,* for permission to quote Kevin's feature on pp 86-90, and for the trust Neil has placed in me. To Dr Barry Rickards who readily gave permission for the quotations from *Angling – Fundamental Principles*. To the suppliers of photographic material, who include those princes among angling photographers Bill Quinlan, Tony Arbery, Bob Buteux, Kevin Clifford and Ron Chant. Then there is the lovely Yvonne Kavanagh, whose drawings and diagrams illustrate the work. I am also grateful to Dr Bruno Broughton, Peter Drennan and Kevin Clifford for their scientific advice and help in various other ways. Finally, to yet another living angling legend, Peter Stone, for supplying the Foreword to this book and, at very short notice, finding the time in his busy schedule to pen the chapter on roach. 'Old Stoney' has retained his love and enthusiasm for big-fish angling for more years than most; long may it remain so.

1
Ecology

In recent times, when the damage being caused to our environment by the twin evils of pollution and industrialisation was finally realised, and thinking 'green' became fashionable, a rallying word to focus public attention was required. Hence, Dr Barry Rickards tells us, 'ecology' was liberated from the strict preserves of the scientist's vocabulary and brought into everyday use.

The origins of the word 'ecology' reach back to the 1800s, when a word was needed by the scientific community to define the study of how animals interact with each other and their environment. The basic tenet of ecology is that life does not exist apart from its environment and that each species is, in fact, a product of its own particular environment or 'eco-system', owing its existence to factors of climate, geography and geology.

Sosin and Clark in their book *Through the Fish's Eye* state that 'Ecology is the dynamic aspect of nature's system. From a standpoint of fishing, it relates each fish to such factors as water conditions, nearby objects, available food, potential enemies, and even the fisherman.'

Moreover, it must be appreciated that a river is a constantly changing environment. And, clearly, these changes are vital to the well-being of its inhabitants. Perhaps the differing amounts of water the river is carrying is its most obvious change, so we will start with this.

Water Levels

Rivers have water levels which rise and fall, and much life in and around the river depends on this fact. Winter's floods, whether they are caused by melting snow or heavy rainfall, are vital to the life of the river. The increase in flow scours away unproductive mud, rubbish and debris, and exposes new unexploited feeding areas for the fish. Sickly and/or weak fish will also not be able to withstand these powerful currents. High water also means that any pollutants present are effectively diluted to less dangerous levels, and extra food for the fish, such as worms and insects, are washed into the river.

Water is such a uniquely powerful solvent that it dissolves and carries numerous substances in solution upon which aquatic life depends. Dissolved oxygen, carbon dioxide, nitrogen, phosphorus, potassium, iron and other chemicals are all found in water. And water rapidly carries away not only solid and liquid, but gaseous wastes as well.

Equally important are the effects of low-water conditions, especially those of summertime. These allow some insects to complete their life-cycle and help the fish to breed successfully. At this time the easy pace of the summer's stream allows the fish to recover as quickly as possible from the effects of strenuous spawning and prevents the resulting fry from being washed away. Summer is also the time when most natural food is available – hence the fish rapidly rebuild their strength, all the better to withstand the floods when they occur.

It would appear that some of the National Rivers Authorities' engineers are oblivious to these facts and assume that as long as the river carries a sufficient amount of water of acceptable quality, all is well. It is up to each and every one of us, as caring anglers, to point out the error of this idea. Undoubtedly, the well-being of the river and its dependent flora and fauna, rely on varying water levels and flow rates, at the appropriate time of the year.

Temperature

As cold-blooded creatures, the body temperature of fish is governed by the temperature of the surrounding

water. Remember, however, that the temperature adjustment is not an instant process and rapid temperature changes may produce fish kills, simply because the fish cannot adjust quickly enough. Fortunately, water temperature does not change as quickly as air. Unlike stillwaters, rivers are usually approximately of the same temperature bed to surface from the effects of constant mixing, whether the water is deep or shallow.

A widely held belief among biologists is that temperature is the single most important factor governing the occurrence and behaviour of fish. Research on fish demonstrates that heat accelerates the life processes. For example, trout use four times as much oxygen in warm water as they do in cold water. To survive, fish may need twice as much oxygen in water over 65°F as they would if the water were 40°F. Carp digest their food four times as fast at 79°F than they do at 50°F.

● *The Royalty Fishery, bank-high in winter*

Oxygen Limitations

In order to survive, fish must have abundant dissolved oxygen in the waters in which they live, so oxygen is a critical ecological limitation. Oxygen gets into the water either from the air above the surface or from the plant life below it. The air also acts as a buffer in the other direction, absorbing oxygen from the water should saturation levels be too high.

The air we breathe is 18 per cent oxygen, but fish must exist by breathing in water that, on average, contains only .0006 per cent oxygen (six parts dissolved oxygen per million parts of water). When the dissolved oxygen content is diminished below the normal amount by around 25 per cent, fish have trouble with feeding, growth, self-protection and other vital activities. If dissolved oxygen is lowered by around 50 per cent or more, the fish die from suffocation. Such is the thin line between all being well and certain catastrophe.

Water Clarity

Silt adversely affects the aquatic habitat because it affects the clarity of the water. Sunlight is screened preventing photosynthesis, and when silt settles on the bottom it smothers plants and destroys delicate aquatic creatures, including the spawn of some fish. It has been demonstrated that clear water is thirteen times as productive as coloured water.

Some fish bite poorly in coloured water – for example, chub and pike. An American biologist, G. W.

Bennet, who measures water transparency using a small white disc (Secci disc), says in his book *Management of Lakes and Ponds* that 'In most small lakes and ponds, fishing is poor if the transparency of the water is less than two feet.'

Productivity

It has long been realised that whatever its size, a shallow lake is more productive acre by acre than a deep one. For similar reasons, narrow streams are more productive acre for acre than wide rivers, particularly

● *Jack Hilton fishing a very productive southern river, the Dorset Stour*

if they are clear. This is simply because sunlight can penetrate to the bottom more readily, warming the water in the process. Also, clarity enhances productivity because clear, silt-free water allows maximum sunlight penetration.

If you bear the foregoing in mind, you can easily understand why waters occurring within regions enjoying longer hours of daylight are usually best at producing more and bigger fish. Water temperature comes into this as well, of course; the longer the period of suitable – that is, warm conditions – the longer the growing season. Hence, it is not surprising that most of the more prolific and productive of Britain's waters are situated in the South.

Tidal Water

To the angler who fishes tidal water, tides are not only important but they may be critical to success. Many areas only contain fish on a certain stage of the tide and then only for an hour or two. For the rest of the time, the entire area may be devoid of fish, or it may seem that way. Generally speaking, if fish are found at a particular place at a particular time, and conditions such as weather or temperature don't fluctuate too much, the chances are that they will be found there again the next day, except that they will turn up an hour later – the time of the next day's tide.

Tides are caused by the gravitational effect of the moon and the sun, although the latter's effect is insignificant and may be discounted for all practical purposes. On the new and full moons, the tides are somewhat higher and lower than they are at other times of the month. In some places, fishing will be found to be better during these periods because the fish can sometimes take advantage of feeding in areas they cannot reach under normal tidal conditions. Therefore, not only are the times of the tides important, but the tidal range can be equally important.

Barometric Pressure

I have been unable to define the effect of barometric pressure on the feeding of fish, but have no doubt that it does exert influence. Gerry Swanton agrees, because he has stated that 'Barometric pressure has great bearing on the feeding of roach'. Similarly, Barry Rickards in his book *Angling Fundamental Principles*, says, 'And then I began, vaguely, to think about barometric pressure. I think it first occurred to me on one of those oppressive days when you feel lethargic – when the pressure of the air is low and you get less oxygen per breath into your lungs. If not me, why not the fish?'

A Practical Experiment

In recent years, one of the big questions concerning the well-being of the Hampshire Avon is why there are so few small, immature fish coming through to replace the larger specimens as these die off. Most Avon authorities seem to think that the lack of roach in such sizes is the worst affected species, so let us examine a likely scenario.

It is now well known that there are, throughout the Avon Valley, many trout farms utilising the river's water, and some of these farms have been in existence for many years. About twenty or thirty years ago, control of these farms was much less strict than it is today and many thousands of trout were allowed to escape into the river. Now it is realised that fish are ready to exploit any glut of available food, and Avon pike are no exception. Consequently, the pike population grew to excessive proportions on a rich diet of fresh rainbow trout. Later, when controls on trout farms were tightened up and massive escapes became a thing of the past, pike had to look to other species to sustain their appetite in order to survive. This fact may well account for the lack of immature roach, etc, and the longer the situation is allowed to go on unchecked, the more serious the problem will become.

I have heard the argument that it is not the pike but the trout escapees themselves that are eating the immature fish. This argument may sound plausible at first, but this theory has been disproved by a demonstration that proved that trout eat very few immature fish.

Mike Trowbridge, the Head Riverkeeper of Lord Radnor's Longford Estate, which has several miles of the Hampshire Avon flowing through it, has long recognised the problem. For the last five years or so, Mike has been trying to do something about it by, among other things, artificially rearing roach.

Like most good river-keepers, Mike is an excellent

● *Electro fishing can be a vital component of fishery management*

and gifted naturalist. From his observations he noted that roach preferred one of the common water mosses, fontinalis, in which to deposit their spawn. Mike nailed fontinalis to boards which he then placed in the river in known roach spawning areas. It was then a simple matter of observation and checking to ensure that the boards were collected at the right time – that is, when the fontinalis contained masses of roach eggs.

The spawn-laden fontinalis was then carefully removed from the boards and placed in special holding tanks. When the eggs hatched, the resultant fry were fed on a mixture containing dried hard-boiled egg-yolk. Then, when big enough, the immature roach were moved to previously prepared ponds. These ponds had been manured before flooding to encourage a heavy alga bloom by summer. The algae provide a natural and ready available source of food for the young fish. By the following summer the roach were of a size to be self-sufficient and they were then returned to the river. All

the processes were carried out using River Avon water, which had no extra treatment or purification. And there are, of course, sewerage-treatment plants and other trout farms, besides all the main tributaries, situated above Longford in the valley. Therefore, water quality does not seem to be a major cause affecting the occurrence of roach in the Hampshire Avon. But Mike does believe that a break in the food-chain could be a contributory factor.

There is no doubt that Mike's experiments in propagating roach fry have been successful, which the members of the syndicate who fish the Longford Estate will recognise, for in the Longford waters there now is no shortage of immature roach, or even mature roach. As

● *Mike Trowbridge is steadying the boat while Bob James poses with a big roach from the Longford Estate waters of the Hampshire Avon*

a graphic example, Bob James' big catch of specimen roach, mentioned in the Preface and illustrated on the front cover, was caught from the Longford waters.

Another possible factor in the Avon roach decline may be the destruction of the river's water-meadow and carrier system. These carriers provided a constant sheltered environment for immature fish, and, as they are alternately flooded one year and left to dry the next, they provided enrichment and extra food. With this thought in mind, Longford rods, Hugh Miles and Bob James, have introduced the Longford Conservation Fund. All monies raised by the fund are used towards paying for the restoration of the estate's carrier and water-meadow system. Within twelve months of the scheme's introduction, more than 2 miles of dilapidated carriers have been restored.

● *Longford Castle provides an impressive back-drop to Hugh Miles' roach swim*

Another factor in the decline of the Hampshire Avon is highlighted by Mike's success – the lack of professional water-keepers on the river. Up until about the time of World War II, the Avon then, as now, ran almost exclusively through private estates. Nowadays, however, most of the riparian owners cannot afford to employ an army of professional water-keepers, as in the past. And even if, by some miracle, they could again afford the money, the problem has now been exacerbated by the fact that most of the traditional river-keepers are now dead, and all the water lore passed down through countless generations has died with them. All we can do is to be grateful for the few river-keepers who survive, especially those of the calibre of Mike Trowbridge.

As the old saying goes, 'It's an ill wind that blows nobody any good', and perhaps the severe reduction in numbers of coarse fish in the Avon has resulted in a lack of competition for the available food. This, then, seems a likely contributing factor why the fish that do survive

have a better chance of growing much quicker and, ultimately, of being far heavier as a result. Personally, I believe that this is one of the main factors why there are now more very large fish in the Avon than for many years. There certainly are more big fish now than at any time during my lifetime; this not only applies to roach, but to big chub and big barbel as well; the Royalty Fishery at Christchurch, however, is a special case.

The Royalty Fishery

A cursory glance at the list of the biggest barbel caught in Britain clearly illustrates the supremacy that the Royalty Fishery once held for this species. It is not clear why this occurred, but the following will explain most of the reasons.

It is general knowledge that the Avon's initial barbel stock came from the Thames, which was caught and transferred in 1896 by a London angler, a Mr Gomm. This first batch, consisting of about a hundred fish, were stocked at Iford Bridge on the Dorset Stour. As the

● *Bill Keal fishes the famed Railway Pool on the Royalty Fishery*

Stour shares an estuary with the Avon at Christchurch, it was not long before some of the barbel colonised the Avon, too. These first barbel migrants into the Avon had advantages that precious few fish enjoy. Simply that they were the *first* barbel in these sweet waters was their initial advantage.

At the same time, it is known that, to prevent themselves outgrowing their environment, fish excrete certain chemicals (called pheromones) which, when they reach sufficient strength in the water, reduce or, in extreme cases, prevent growth. It follows, therefore, that if one particular group is the first of a species to inhabit a large stretch of water like the Avon, there is little chance that the levels of dilution will affect growth at all, especially when it is remembered that none of the Avon's tributaries contained barbel either. This meant that the water flowing down to the new residents was uncontaminated by this means, too.

A hundred years ago, the Avon was contaminated by little else which might adversely affect the barbel. Trout hatcheries which, in some experts' opinions, are the major polluters of the river today, were more or less unknown and chemical fertilisers were much less used by farmers than they are now. Remember, too, that any pollutants were there in much weaker dilutions, because water abstraction had not reached anything like today's level. Many more millions of gallons of water flowed down the Avon in any given year then than in a similar period now.

At the same time, it is difficult to imagine a more perfect habitat for barbel than that which existed on the Royalty when those first barbel arrived. The bed is nearly all gravel, with plenty for all. On the other hand, as barbel do not seem to like bright light, one could be forgiven for thinking that the crystal-clear water of the river in summer would be a distinct disadvantage. But that was not so, for the extremely profuse summer weed-growth provided (and still provides) the ideal sanctuary from the sun that the barbel need. And, apart from providing protection, those same weed-beds also provide food.

Of further significance, however, is the fact that, in addition to the abundant natural larder the Royalty waters provided, there were two other sources of easily obtainable nourishment, and it is these which sets apart the Royalty from any other section of the Avon.

First and adjacent to what is now known as the Bridge Pool, a slaughterhouse once stood. It takes little imagination to guess that the unsold offal was deposited in the river, and that the blood was hosed in, too. With such easy pickings available, one might wonder why the barbel ventured upstream at all, but they did

have a reason. A century ago, on the site at the top of the Parlour Pool (now the West Hampshire Water Company's works), there was a water-mill that ground locally grown products into flour. It would be no exaggeration to surmise that, during this period, tons of flour and grain found its way into the river from this source alone, for then, as now, the river flows right through the building. So, with meat from the abattoir, flour and grain from the mill, as well as the river's own prolific natural menu, it is not surprising that the Royalty produced the biggest barbel in the land.

Until after World War II, the Royalty barbel were largely unmolested by anglers. While many of the really big fish were caught before this time, relatively few anglers fished this water then. My information is that only four coarse fishermen were allowed on the water at any given time. I make this point because any animal that is continually afraid to eat is not going to grow quickly. In other words, fish that are often caught are sooner or later going to become very careful feeders.

Obviously, other species – notably chub – thrived on the conditions that prevailed early in the Royalty's history. A string of 7-pounders were recorded in the early years of the present century, culminating in the record 8lb 4oz chub, caught by G. F. Smith in 1913, which remains at the head of the current list. Although the Royalty was undoubtedly 'something special' in those days, I do not want to give the impression that it is now finished as one of our premier fisheries. Nothing could be further from the truth. For example, specimens taken from the Royalty this current season (1991–2) include 12lb+ barbel, 6lb 7oz chub, 30lb+ pike and 30lb+ carp. If you know of a water with returns better than this, can I persuade you to tell me about it!

2
Recognition

Before you start to fish the rivers of England, it might be a good idea to give an indication of what species you are likely to catch. This might sound a simple enough task, yet a complete description would alone fill a book twice the size of this one. From necessity, therefore, this chapter will not be a complete catalogue; there will, however, be enough information to satisfy all but the most demanding anglers.

Around the turn of the century the 'Trent Otter' reported that the River Trent's name is derived from an ancient word meaning thirty. Martin concluded that this suggests that the Trent, at some time in the past, sustained no less than thirty different species of fish. He may or may not have been correct in his assumption, but I do know that there are still enough different species of fish in our rivers to satisfy most tastes and anglers of all ages and experience.

Recognising the various species is mostly straightforward, although you will have to look more carefully to distinguish, say, the silver bream from an immature specimen of its near relative, the common bream. And, of course, it is important to know that the big roach you have caught really is a roach and not something else, such as a roach/bream hybrid. The problem of hybridisation is a difficult one, and even if you go to the ultimate length of an autopsy, you may still not be 100 per cent certain. Therefore, as angling is not an exact science, all we can do on the riverbank is to try to be as sure as we can that a particular fish is what we say it is. To do this, we must take care to observe and note all the

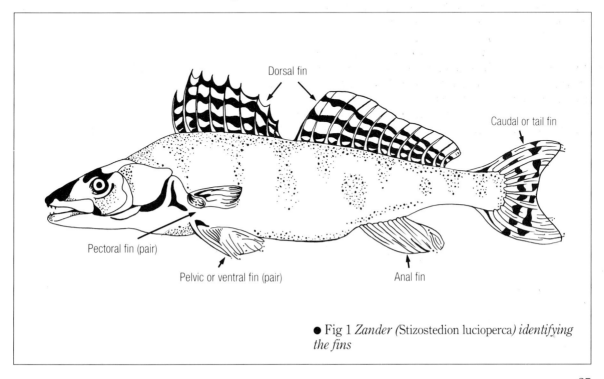

● Fig 1 *Zander (*Stizostedion lucioperca*) identifying the fins*

physical characteristics, such as scale and fin-ray counts. Good-quality, close-up photographs, taken at the time of capture, will also be useful to experts on hybridisation, should the need arise – say, in the event of a possible 'record' or prize-winning fish.

I will begin by describing the smallest fish I have caught.

Miller's Thumb or Bullhead (*Cottus gobio*)

The name 'miller's thumb' is derived from its flat appearance (miller's thumbs were said in days of old to be flat after years of feeling the texture of flour). It is a bottom-living fish, with a large, wide, flat head, from which a sharp spine projects backwards on either side. The pelvic fins are light coloured and unmarked; the inner ray is about half the length of the longest rays. It is an ugly customer: dirty green in colour, mottled from olive to black, and it rarely grows longer than 4½–5in. It lives on a stony bottom in fairly shallow water and is easily found by lifting stones or rocks. The miller's thumb has no swim bladder, is slow moving, and is easily caught by hand. It makes a useful bait for perch, etc.

Stone Loach (*Nemacheilus barbatulus*) Spined Loach (*Cobitis taenia*)

The two species of loach found in England are both found in clear, fast, pebbly streams, and may be caught in the same way as the miller's thumb. The loaches look something like gudgeon, but are more slender. Their average length is 3in. The more common of the two is the stone loach, which has a straight-ended tail. The spined loach gets its name from the movable double spine below each eye; this and its convex tail differentiate it from the stone loach. Both are mottled in appearance and have six small barbels around the mouth. The stone loach is perhaps bigger than the spined loach. They make excellent baits for perch, etc, and I know of at least one river tench being caught on a stone loach live-bait.

Ruffe or Pope (*Gymnocephalus cernua*)

Although I seldom deliberately fish for ruffe or pope, I have caught plenty of this poor relation of the perch in the Thames, but seldom anywhere else. Unlike the perch, the ruffe has no vertical stripes (its colour being mottled dirty greyish-brown), and its double dorsal fin is joined at the centre. In angling, the ruffe has no particular value and is often considered a nuisance when it takes the bait, usually worm or maggot, that was meant for more worthy adversaries. It rarely exceeds 6in in length.

Gudgeon (*Gobio gobio*)

Considering its small size – a good one weighs 3oz – the gudgeon puts up a remarkably good fight when hooked. In appearance it resembles a miniature barbel, although it possesses only two barbels (barbel usually have four – more on this later). Some anglers confuse gudgeon with the loaches, but its forked tail is a sure giveaway. They feed voraciously on anything that is available, as long as it is near the bottom, both in winter and summer. Its natural diet consists of the larvae of insects, worms, crustaceans, and occasionally fish eggs, sucked in by its protractile mouth. The best baits include small pieces of redworm, bloodworm and maggot. Because of their availability, maggots are the gudgeon's most popular food source.

The gudgeon is greenish-brown in colour and its flanks are often marked with a line of black or bluish spots, although this colouration depends a lot on its environment. Many years ago I kept gudgeon for baits in an old white enamelled bath; the longer they were kept in this receptacle the paler they became, and they also lost their characteristic spots. Despite this colour change, their effectiveness as baits was not diminished. Perch, pike and trout all eat gudgeon.

Bleak (*Alburnas alburnas*)

The bleak can be important to the match angler, for it

is relatively easy to catch where it is present in large numbers. Expert Thames matchmen used to catch bleak at the rate of up to four hundred an hour. I say 'used to' because the vast shoals of bleak, once so prolific in the Thames, now seem a thing of the past.

Bleak rarely weigh more than a few ounces at best and they are sometimes mistaken for immature dace. The anal fin is the distinguishing feature: this fin is much longer in the bleak, the base of which is longer than the dorsal fin. The reverse is true of the dace.

The bleak is an important food source for perch, pike, zander and other predators. Therefore its value as a bait should not be underestimated. Its own food consists of water-fleas, bloodworm, pupae of gnats, etc and flying insects. It feeds at or near the surface.

A deadly method of catching bleak in the summertime is to throw in frequently light cloud ground-bait, laced with maggot and/or casters. When a shoal of bleak takes advantage of this free feast, a single maggot or caster bait is cast among it. The smallest, lightest self-cocking float, with the minimum of shot down the line, or none at all if you can get away with it, is usually the correct rig. In summer the fish will rarely feed more than 3ft beneath the surface, and a slowly sinking bait set at that depth will save you the trouble of determining exactly what the feeding depth is. Bleak bite rapidly, so you will have to have your wits about you. A refinement is to crinkle the line between the hook and float and watch for the crinkles to straighten out. This tactic increases the catch rate dramatically, because when the bleak encounters resistance of the float, it lets go immediately.

Dace (Sometimes Dart or Graining) (*Leuciscus leuciscus*)

We have seen already how to differentiate between bleak and dace, and recognising the difference between dace and chub is even easier. Again, it is the anal fin that gives the game away: on the dace the edge of this fin is concave, whereas the chub's anal fin is convex. The dace can also resemble a slender roach, but the eyes are yellowish (never red like a roach's), and the iris has small dark spots. The body is bright silver in colour and the fins have either a yellowish or greenish tinge.

The dace has 47–54 scales along the lateral line to the

chub's 42–9 and 40–6 of the roach. This may help to determine the species since the dace only overlaps by two scales with the chub and does not come in the same range as the roach. A 1lb dace is a specimen from any water.

Big Thames dace are seemingly rare these days, whereas the chalk streams of the South all produce beautiful specimen fish, as do the chalk or part-chalk rivers of Bedfordshire and Hertfordshire. The Ivel and the Beane both have reputations for producing fine dace. The rivers Evenlode, Gipping, Medway, Great Ouse, Soar, Dorset Stour, Suffolk Stour, Swale, Tees and Tone have all produced good dace in recent years.

Dace will feed at all levels from bottom to surface, but, remember, they bite very fast and let go even quicker. In floodwater, they will be found generally close to the bottom. At such times worm, maggots or bread, fished on leger tackle, is best. Light float tackle is preferable when the water is less heavy, which will give better results. For summertime fishing, my own tackle choice is a Drennan 12ft Chrystalight rod, a 2lb bs Double-Strength main-line, with a 1lb hook-link of the same material, and fine wire hooks in sizes 12–18. Dace have exceptionally good eyesight, so keep a low profile and long-trot, say, a light stick-float, using either a single maggot or caster, or a fragment of bread-crust on the hook.

Roach (*Rutilus rutilus*)

If Dick Walker was restricted to fishing for one species of fish he would have picked roach, and he is not alone in this choice. The roach has been one of the most popular species for generations of Britain's anglers, a trend which continues for some until the present day.

In appearance the roach varies very much according to its environment. But a typical fish would have large silver scales, tinged with metallic green to the back, and shot with metallic blue to the flanks. The fins are reddish, as are the eyes. An imaginary vertical line drawn from the root of the front ray of the dorsal fin would also approximately bisect the same place on the first ray of the pelvic fins. This relationship of the beginning of the dorsal fin, immediately above the start of the pelvics, is an important point in identifying the roach. For example, the dorsal fin of the rudd is set much nearer the tail than the pelvics. Another important

● *Roach (*Rutilus rutilus*)*

difference between roach and rudd is the shape of the mouth: in the roach the top lip overlaps the lower one, while the opposite occurs in the rudd.

As has already been intimated, dorsal and anal fin-ray counts, and longitudinal and transverse scale counts are essential features of identification in fish. The dorsal fin of the roach has 3 soft, unbranched rays and between 9 and 11 branched rays, and the anal fin likewise. A longitudinal count, taken along the lateral line, may show between 40 and 46 scales, but most commonly 42 or 43. In the transverse series, there are normally 7 above the lateral line and 5 below.

The late David Carl Forbes, in his classic book *Successful Roach Fishing*, had this to say about roach:

The lateral line, which is complete from gill-cover to the root of the tail, may be made up of between 40 and 46 scales, although I have yet to encounter a specimen with more than 44 scales along this line and, from research I am currently carrying out, it could well prove that the numerical range of scales is somewhat smaller than is normally quoted. One popular book of European freshwater fish quotes as many as 49 scales along the lateral line, but I would be wary indeed of a roach with such a count. Random counts on British roach over two or three seasons have yet to show a specimen with more than 43 scales along the lateral line, but much more work is required before any definite conclusions can be drawn from this.

David Carl Forbes was unable to complete his research, for he was tragically killed in a motoring accident.

Then there is the question of hybridisation, for roach have been known to interbreed with several other species, notably bleak, rudd and bream. Also, I am told that roach/chub hybrids are not uncommon in the Trent. In some cases trained observers have also reported mixtures of characteristics from more than two species. Understandably, then, it is almost impossible to be 100 per cent sure of what is a true roach, assuming, of course, that such a creature actually exists. Remember that even if the fish was killed, dissected and examined under a microscope, the result is still not absolutely conclusive. Should I ever be fortunate enough to capture an enormous roach, I would take the following steps to be as sure as possible of its identity (under no circumstances would I kill it):

1 Record scale and fin-ray counts.
2 Take a number of excellent photographs, including close-ups of the mouth, anal fin and tail. Some at least should show the relative positions between pelvic and dorsal fins.
3 Get an acknowledged expert on hybridisation to see the fish. Three names that spring to mind are Kevin Clifford, Neville Fickling and Alwyne Wheeler.
4 If you cannot get an expert to see the fish, send copies of the photographs (not negatives in case they are lost), to either or all of the previously named gentlemen. Contact may be made through the National Association of Specialist Anglers (NASA) or the angling press.

The roach is one of the most numerous and common fish in British waters, not just rivers, and by its very abundance is an important aspect in the ecology of these waters. It preys on larvae, although its main food is comprised of vegetable matter. It is itself preyed on by larger fish, such as pike, zander, perch and, to some extent, eels. Therefore, it makes a good bait for predatory fish, but is difficult to transport and keep alive. Remember that it is an offence to move fish from one water to another without proper authorisation.

Roach breed prolifically in most rivers, tolerating high levels of pollution. Its abundance and its other attributes make it most important to anglers.

The size roach attain is dependent on its environment. Where overcrowding occurs, roach often only attain a length of 4–6in. In good growing conditions, however, a length of 16–18in may be attained. The best big roach environments exist on those princely southern rivers – the Hampshire Avon and the Dorset Stour. Indeed, the current British record roach was caught

from the Stour in 1990. An account of the capture of this specimen is told by its captor, Ray Clarke, in Chapter 11.

For most anglers, a 2lb roach is regarded as a specimen; however, dyed-in-the-wool roach specialists seek fish at least 50 per cent heavier than this. Such is the situation that presently exists, that this is not as hopeless a target as it once was, for, like many other species, there are probably more big roach in our rivers than at any time before, and, certainly during my lifetime.

Chub (sometimes Chevin, Chavender, or Loggerhead) (*Leuciscus cephalus*)

Remembering that the chub's anal fin is convex should enable you to identify members of this species readily. However, other features are equally distinctive: the chub has a large head (hence loggerhead), a large mouth, white leathery lips and gold-flecked eyes. Despite all these obvious points of recognition, it would not be the first time that a glass-cased specimen 'roach' has proved to be a chub. Unfortunately, a scale count is not conclusive. The chub has 42–9 scales along the lateral line, and the transverse count, from the root of the dorsal fin to the lateral line, is 7–8. Chub scales are very large – much larger than those of the roach – and are edged with black. Both the dorsal and anal fins have 7–9 branched rays.

The chub's natural diet is composed of flying insects, all kinds of water insect, slugs, worms, molluscs, fish eggs, and often plants and seeds. When they grow big, chub will often become more predatory and feed on larger animals, particularly fish, frogs, tadpoles, etc. Their feeding habits vary: almost any bait, from bread to boilies, from spinner to the most sophisticated dry-fly, all these and plenty of others, catch chub. The chub is an enigma, showing extreme caution on one occasion and feeding with gay abandon on another. It will rush at a well-presented bait, but will flee at a careless footfall.

During the early part of the season, larger chub enjoy live fish meals, not excluding their own offspring. Sometimes they are shoal fish, at other times loners; it may be more accurate to say that they become more solitary as they grow bigger.

● *Chub (Leuciscus cephalus) are great confidence-boosters*

In the summertime, chub are frequently found under trees or bushes waiting for insects to fall, or adjacent to weed-beds foraging for anything that the current may bring down to them. They will feed at all levels from bottom to surface. In the winter they stay much nearer the bottom as a rule, and legering the deeper water is a reliable method at this time. They can be most difficult to tempt in coloured water, (see pp 75-6).

Izaac Walton's description of the chub as 'the fearfullest of fishes' is so apt that most other writers on chub ever since have quoted him. It is best to approach chub swims as quietly and as slowly as possible. Ensuring that your shadow does not fall upon the water and keeping a low profile will also help, as will making use of any natural cover.

Chub, provided they are big, are one of my favourite species. Bob Buteux, one of the most successful catchers of big chub, used to fish throughout the season for the species. His most successful season during 1964–5 saw him land seven specimens over 4lb each. As an example of how things have changed, in a single weekend during the 1990–1 winter, Bob caught no less than nine 4-pounders. All were caught on bread-flake!

The universal specialist chub man's ambition is to catch a 5-pounder, and that is a good and realistic target. It is not too difficult to achieve, provided that you fish the right rivers, of course, and yet it is not so easy either. Until very recently, a 6-pounder was considered in the 'fish of a lifetime' category but, with each passing season, it seems that the chance of catching such a specimen improves. Every season chub of this size are reported from many parts of the country, although the majority of such fish come from southern rivers.

The record chub was caught from the Hampshire Avon, at Christchurch, in December 1913. The fortunate fisherman was a Mr G. F. Smith, from Putney, south-west London. This leviathan weighed no less than 8lb 4oz. However, you may wonder how this particular record has survived for so long if chub are getting bigger year by year. Well, as explained in Chapter 1, a special case existed on the Royalty Fishery. The Avon was then much less tainted by the effluent from fish-farms and other pollutants, so its waters were much purer and sweeter than they are today. Also, there was more water – nowadays, abstraction, drawn off higher up the valley, ensures that much less water flows down the Avon. Furthermore, at Christchurch were two important sources of food for the chub that have long since disappeared: what is now the West Hampshire Water Works pumping station was then a working mill, so a great deal of grain would have found its way into the river. Then, down in the town itself, a slaughterhouse stood on the bank. The easiest and cheapest way of disposing the offal was to throw it in the river. The chub loved it, of course, and waxed fat as a result; moreover, Mr G. F. Smith's huge chub was caught at that very spot.

I do not believe that the chub record is unbeatable. In fact, in the light of what we are experiencing in the potential increase in the size of chub, it would not surprise me if the chub record is soon eclipsed, as long as the rivers are not decimated by pollution in the meantime.

Perch (*Perca fluvilatilus*)

Perch cannot be confused with any other species, with the possible exception of its poor relation, the ruffe. The

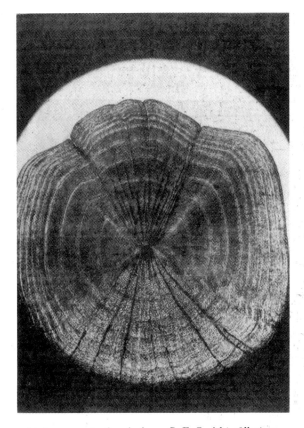

● *Enlargement of scale from G. F. Smith's 8lb 4oz record chub. Caught from the Royalty on 16 December 1913, on pith – ie, beef marrow*

body of the perch is hump-backed and is marked with five or six vertical black stripes. It has a double dorsal fin, of which the two components are separated by a gap. The front dorsal fin has thirteen to fifteen very sharp spines and is marked with a black area at or near the rear. Also, the rear of the gill covers are armed with a strong spike.

The top of the back is almost black, shading through to green on the flanks, and is yellowish-white on the belly. The tail and under-fins are a rich red. There are, however, considerable colour variations, perhaps depending upon the fish's environment.

The perch is a fierce predator and is not immune from consuming its own young. In fact, most of the large perch caught by my friends and myself, were taken on tiny perch live-baits (in our defence, it was a very long time ago). They will also eat anything meaty; lobworms

31

are probably the most successful bait, with maggots a close second, especially for smaller fish.

Perch lie in ambush for their prey, and their striped colouration is a natural camouflage. As they are only able to make short bursts of speed, the target is attacked from behind. Some authorities state that the victim's tail is attacked first to prevent it escaping, then it is swallowed head-first. Perch are active all year and are more likely to seek out deeper-water in the colder months.

The mid-1960s saw a decline in the numbers of perch and many authorities believed that they were the victims of a disease. Personally, I am not sure that this was the reason, but I do remember, at that time, seeing many large containers, each full of dead perch, being removed from the Barn Elms reservoirs. The situation now appears much improved and perch, especially big ones, are making a welcome reappearance. This, though, could be a case of anglers discovering new stocks that somehow avoided the ravages of the disease rather than the perch making a concerted come-back. But I sincerely hope that they are returning in strength. A realistic target weight for perch is 2lb, but, undoubtedly, much bigger specimens exist in our rivers.

Silver Bream (*Blicca bjoernka*) Common Bream (*Abramis brama*)

There are two kinds of bream in British waters: the silver (or white) and the common (or bronze), and much confusion exists as to how to differentiate between the two. Like Peter Stone, I don't worry too much about the problem, for silver bream are quite rare. I don't know whether I have ever caught one and I am sure that I don't care. They don't grow very big – one weighing 1lb would be a specimen – whereas the common variety can weigh considerably more. Both species have a compressed body shape; the common bream has a pronounced hump-back and is very deep bodied.

When adult, the silver bream is bright silver in colour, which alone should make identification straightforward. Immature specimens can be differentiated by the following means: the anal fin of the silver bream is shorter than the common bream's and has 19–24 branched rays; the common bream's anal fin has 23–9 branched rays. Furthermore, there are 8–11 scales in a transverse line between the dorsal fin and the lateral line in the silver bream and 11–15 in the common species. The scale count along the lateral line is less conclusive, being 43–55 in the silver variety and 49–57 in the common. Perhaps the most easily recognised difference between the two species is eye size. The eye of the silver bream is either greater in diameter or as long as its snout. The common bream's eye is always smaller than the length of its snout.

Common bream are numerous in slow-moving reaches of rivers, although one of the biggest river-caught specimens I know of came from the middle reaches of the Hampshire Avon. Ron Chant was its captor and it weighed 9lb 14oz.

Bream are confirmed bottom feeders and they will eat almost any aquatic insect; worms and maggots are therefore the best baits. Bread-paste is also good, as is sweetcorn at times. At night bream often move into the margins or on to the shallows to feed. As they are gregarious, large quantities of ground-bait are required to keep a shoal of bream interested. For all practical purposes, legering is *the* method to take bream.

As most river bream are slimy and, in my opinion, don't fight well, they are one of my least favourite river fish, but they rate highly with match anglers. A 3–4lb line and a size 12–14 hook will adequately handle even the biggest bream as long as you can control yourself sufficiently not to break off on the strike.

Pike (*Esox leucius*)

As pike is unique in British waters, it cannot be confused with any other fish. It has a flat broad snout and an extremely large mouth, which is capacious enough to engulf a prey half its own size, although its food items are invariably much smaller. The dorsal and anal fins are of a similar shape and situated close to the tail. This arrangement is the pike's means of rapid acceleration, aided, of course, by its elongated and streamlined body shape.

Male pike do not grow as fast or as big as females, the

● *Terry Lampard and the beautiful barbel known as Henrietta. Note the black mark under the right eye which aids in the identification of this particular fish (*Terry Lampard*)*

BARBEL (British Rod-Caught Record)
Caught by A.D. TRYON in the AVON at Christchurch 1933. Weight...

CHUB
Caught by C.F. SMITH in the River at ...church Dec 16th 1913. Weight 8lbs 4oz...

latter maturing at between 3 and 5 years, the males perhaps a year earlier. River pike sometimes attain weights in excess of 35lb, such specimens invariably being females.

After the first year of life, the pike's diet consists almost completely of fish – dace, roach, rudd, perch and eels. Neither are pike averse to consuming smaller members of their family. Several instances have been recorded of two pike of almost equal size being found dead, one jammed in the mouth of the other. I suggest that this may not be a deliberate act but an accident, and offer this explanation: two pike dash at the same bait fish, from opposing directions, and end up locked in each other's jaws.

The noted Victorian ichthyologist, Frank Buckland, described the pike's mouth thus:

> There are three plates of teeth in the back upper jaw, all of which are needle sharp, and set directly backwards. The lower jaw is also armed with a formidable set of lancet-pointed teeth, so that it is impossible for any object once impacted in a pike's mouth ever to get back out again.

Pike are usually of a greenish hue and marked with primrose-coloured spots or blotches. The fins are either dark red or brown, marked with black. The eyes are large and can look forward for binocular vision – a tremendous asset for this fierce predator.

Pike feed no matter what the water temperature, although it seems clear-water conditions are best for their capture. Every river I have yet fished contains more and bigger pike than most anglers appreciate, which is perhaps surprising, considering the barbaric attitudes of some river-keepers to this splendid fish. In the early 1970s, I can recall seeing piles of dead pike on the floor of the rod-room at the Royalty – a sight which sickened me. River pike are reputed to fight much harder than their stillwater cousins; the story of the capture of my biggest river pike to date should effectively illustrate this (see pp 134–9).

● *The Hon Aylmer Tryon proudly posing with the case containing his 14lb 6oz record barbel, caught from the Royalty Fishery in 1934*

● *After his restoration work on the case, Dave Steuart admires G. F. Smith's 8lb 4oz record chub, caught from the Royalty Fishery in 1913*

Barbel (*Barbus barbus*)

Because this species is arguably the most popular river fish with specialist anglers, it has purposely been left until last.

You cannot confuse the barbel with any other species; the most similar species in appearance is the gudgeon. However, the gudgeon does not grow to more than a few ounces and it is very rare indeed to catch a barbel of similar size, so it is unlikely that you will ever confuse these two fish.

The colouration of barbel varies widely, which is due not just to the effects of its environment; individuals from the same stretch of river, even those caught on the same day and from the same swim, may display quite different colours. A typical example would be light golden-brown on the flanks, shading to a dark greenish-bronze on the back, and creamy-white on the underparts. The dorsal fin is greyish-brown, and the remainder of the fins, sometimes including the tail, are a reddish-orange. When looking for barbel, often the first indication the angler gets is a glimpse of two mighty reddish pectoral fins, sticking out on either side like elephant's ears.

The shape of the tail fin is interesting: the upper lobe is elongated and pointed, and the lower one is distinctly radiused. In days gone by it was suggested that the lower lobe had been rounded by constant rubbing on gravel beds, where barbel love to lie. We now know that the unequal shape of the barbel's tail occurs naturally, as a well-known aquarist, N. E. Perkins, pointed out as long ago as 1955:

> . . . I obtained my first specimen of approximately 1½lb weight for photographic purposes and, on placing it in the aquarium was immediately struck by the unsymmetrical caudal fin and its thickened dorsal margin. Close examination led me to suppose that this was not the result of an accident or past wounds, but that it was a normal feature of the species. Bearing in mind the habits of the fish, this appeared quite a reasonable assumption, since the enlarged upper lobe of the caudal in action would tend to force the head down to the bottom, a position well suited to the ventral mouth and in keeping with well-developed and sensitive barbels . . .

The tail's rounded lower lobe is in proportion with the

barbel's lower fins and it also seems reasonable to me to suppose that the enlarged upper lobe would tend to keep the head downward with the minimum of effort. This, coupled with other features such as an underslung mouth and the shape of the head, with its long tapering snout, confirm that the barbel spends most of its time on or near the bottom.

The dorsal fin has eight branched rays and the anal fin is supposedly convex. I say 'supposedly', for in most of the large specimens examined, the outline of this, and, maybe to a lesser extent, other fins are irregular in shape. In fact, one of the surest ways of identifying

● *Alec Lewis poses with a Stour 20lb+ pike (Alec Lewis)*

● *One of the author's favourite fishing pictures: Kirsty and Kevin Cranstoun proudly pose with a brace of double-figure barbel, caught from the Kennet by their father, Pete (Pete Cranstoun)*

some big individual barbel is by the unique shape of their anal fin.

There are 55–65 scales in the lateral line, while the dorsal fin to the lateral line transverse count is 12–14; these statistics are of academic interest only because, as I have already explained, barbel cannot be confused with any other fish.

Barbel get their name from the huge, well-developed barbels (or barbules) around the mouth. There are usually four (sometimes more), two near the front of the snout and one at each corner of the mouth. I first noted that some barbel have more than four barbels over twenty-five years ago. This was at the time when I first became interested in, and realised the importance of, recognising individual barbel.

In most cases the extra barbel, or barbels, emanate at the root of another, although in some examples a barbel may be branched. Later, I read that a noted Victorian ichthyologist (possibly Francis Day) had also noted that barbel did not necessarily have only four barbels. Recently, it has been suggested that this phenomenor was not noticed until 1986 and that the extensive use of luncheon-meat as bait for barbel has been the cause of the 'extra' barbels. I utterly refute this unsupported supposition, for as anyone can readily appreciate, extra

• *Note the 'branched' barbel (left rear) on this fish caught by Bob Buteux, from the Railway Pool, Royalty Fishery, in the early 1970s*

barbels have existed for much longer than luncheon-meat has been extensively used as bait. The photograph (below) shows a 9lb+ Royalty barbel complete with a branched barbel. This specimen was taken from the Railway Pool by Bob Buteux in 1971, long before luncheon-meat was popular as bait. In fact, Peter Wheat's classic book *The Fighting Barbel*, published in 1967, does not even mention luncheon-meat.

An 8lb barbel is reckoned to be a very good fish from any water (I am certainly happy to catch them this size); a 'double' is a specimen in anyone's book, but with so many huge barbel being captured these days, a 12-pounder is a realistic, if still difficult target. To achieve such a weight, a 12lb barbel has had to survive, in a suitable environment, for around twelve years (we know this from reading its scales). The late Percy Austin was an expert reader of scales and he left us much useful information, among which is his work on the growth rates of barbel. From the *Anglers' News* (13 January 1956), Percy has this to say about barbel:

At 1½ years old (two summers) the average barbel weighs 10oz, at 3 years 1½lb, at 5 years 2¾lb, at 7 years 4¼lb, at 9 years 6½lb, at 11 years 10lb, and after that weights show a considerable variation. One of 12lb 14oz was 12 years, and the largest specimen, killed by otters in December 1952, was 12½ years old. The carcass of this hen fish weighed 14½lb and it was estimated 1½lb had been eaten. This would make the live weight 15¾lb. The last year's growth had been rapid which indicated that it may have had several more years to live.

The oldest fish of which I have record was 11lb 11oz from the same river. It was 14 years plus, in poor condition and growth had been little for the last two years. Until I receive scales from an older barbel I believe that 15 years may be the maximum for this species.

With all due respect to Percy Austin, it is now well understood that barbel, and indeed most other fish, do *not* die at the end of the growing period. Like most other animals, once growing has ceased they live for a considerable period of time until their eventual death. To illustrate, let me relate the following pertinent example.

● *This late 1960s Royalty fish has an extra barbel. It was caught by Bill Quinlan*

In the winter of 1975–6 I caught a 9lb barbel from the Kennet. It was a distinctive individual with a deformed tail that was much too small for its size. Almost exactly ten years later I was on hand to witness the capture of this same fish by Ron Chant. At this later capture its weight had dropped by 4oz to 8lb 12oz. Obviously, this individual was at least 20 years old when it was caught by Ron. What is more, this particular barbel's portrait appeared in the angling press from time to time, long after it was captured by Ron. This is yet another reason to treat with utmost respect the fish we catch. The chances are that an extra large specimen is older than its captor – unless, that is, the captor is older than Bob Buteux.

Do not put barbel in keep-nets because their fins have a tendency to get caught in the mesh, and sometimes it is almost impossible to disentangle them. When a big fish must be retained, it is better to use one of the large keep-sacks or, perhaps better still, a tube, now that these are widely available.

3
Location

Of all the fish found in our rivers, the most popular are roach, chub, barbel and pike, and this chapter will concentrate on these four species which are widely distributed throughout England. Most anglers will not have to travel far in the search of their own particular favourite.

Without doubt, barbel are less widely distributed than roach, chub and pike, yet at least twenty different rivers containing them can readily be brought to mind. Considering the size of the area, perhaps it is the northern angler who has the least choice of barbel waters – the Yorkshire rivers, such as the Ouse, Swale, Ure and Wharfe, etc, are possibly their closest contacts for barbel fishing. The anglers of East Anglia only have the Wensum close at hand, but they do not have to travel far to reach other first-class barbel rivers.

Principal among the barbel rivers of the West are the Severn, Bristol Avon and Wye, and it would not be much of a surprise if the next record came from one of these noble streams. Midland anglers also have a wide and varied choice; rivers in this area include the War-wickshire Avon, the upper reaches of the Severn, the Great Ouse, Teme, and even the mighty Trent, are classic examples.

The southern counties contain much of the cream of barbel fishing. Nevertheless, even though I am a Lon-doner, I still have to travel about a hundred miles to some of the best stretches. Of course, I am not complain-ing – in fact, I have been known to do such a journey three times in one week. The Hampshire Avon and the Dorset Stour will need no introduction to big-fish men, nor does the Kennet or Old Father Thames. There are, however, other less well-known barbel rivers in the South, such as the Middlesex Colne, Holy Brook, Cherwell, etc, all of which are capable of producing very large barbel.

Without exception, the rivers mentioned, as well as many others, contain big fish of other species, so it is not too difficult a task to find a river holding the fish you

seek. However, it may be more of a problem to find just where in the river the big fish for which you yearn spend much of their time.

Discovering waters which provide better-than-aver-age fishing, whether this results in big bags of average-sized fish or fewer but bigger individual fish, is a continual process. You must be constantly alert for any snippet of information, however insignificant it may at first appear, for, added to other clues, it may complete the jigsaw. My own memory is notoriously unreliable, so I make notes on anything to hand at the time, and I then enter them in a book kept specifically for the purpose.

To begin the search for a stretch of river with big fish potential, the angling press has much to offer. Some-times a report will tell you everything, including the water's name. However, this is not usually the case. Usually, the information will be disguised to some extent, which is understandable because a successful angler is not going to give away the location of his 'going' water to just anyone – not especially when he, and perhaps some friends, have spent a great deal of time, money and, most important, effort in discovering the water in the first place. Nevertheless, the necessary information can be pieced together by the ardent angler.

Generally, one of the more reliable sources of infor-mation comes from people with a similar interest. While it is certainly true that you can learn of promising venues from matchmen, pleasure anglers, occasional fishermen and even non-anglers, this is far outweighed by the knowledge which can be provided by other big-fish men. But don't imagine that you can learn every-thing without giving something in return.

Nowadays, throughout the year, there are events at which specialist anglers congregate. The highlight for most is the weekend event, usually held at Lough-borough University, organised by the National Asso-ciation of Specialist Anglers (NASA). At this meeting there are diverse and extremely interesting talks on all aspects of fishing by knowledgeable, successful and enthusiastic anglers. However, to my mind, the most endearing characteristic of the event is the approachability of the successful anglers who attend. All, without exception, will find time for everyone and anyone. The evenings in the bar are enjoyable and, by staying sober, one can learn more in a few hours about big fish and the waters that hold them than in the remainder of the year.

Obviously, checking reports of big-fish producing waters means that you must visit them. The primary aim is to see with your own eyes the size and species of fish you seek whether they are caught or in the water. But even if you don't observe them, all is not lost as there are other factors which suggest the presence and whereabouts in the river of large fish.

The next clues can be learned from the fish themselves. For example, barbel, to all intents and purposes, are confirmed bottom feeders, so, invariably, a bait intended for the species would not be presented anywhere else except on or close to the river-bed. Chub, on the other hand, display no such preference and will feed at any depth from the bottom to the surface. Pike may be considered similar in habit to chub in this respect, and roach akin to barbel. Roach, however, are delicate, gentle creatures, quite unlike the bold, brave barbel, so individuals of these species often prefer differing strengths and speed of current. Roach will seek out areas of quiet, slow water, while barbel will not be deterred by strong currents.

So, even before you visit the river, you are making some sense of the problem of location. Then, when you are actually on the bank, the most reliable evidence of where a fish lives is actually to see it. This is straightforward in clear water, such as exists in summer on rivers such as the Hampshire Avon and the Dorset Stour, but a different situation exists when the water is turbid and you cannot see, even with the undoubted benefit of polarising sunglasses, more than 6in into it. Of course, you can still observe the evidence of fish: barbel, for example, sometimes leap clear of the water, and a big leaping barbel makes such a disturbance that it will hardly pass unnoticed. Similarly, roach sometimes 'prime' on or near the surface. But, even if you can't see any visible signs of the fish, all is not lost.

Location of river fish, when you can't actually see them, is an important aspect, for you can't catch them if they are not there in the first place. Although this statement is elementary, many anglers seem to overlook this vital consideration. The people I am talking about begin the process of location correctly by learning of a stretch of river that produces the sought-after species. Then they seem to lose their way. Some think that all the fish are bunched together and that, no matter what the conditions, a known hot-spot is the only place worth fishing; then there are the anglers who believe that the fish are spread evenly throughout the stretch, rather like currants in a cake. Both these observations are well off the mark.

It is true, of course, that in any given piece of water there will be hot-spots and that these will more likely produce a catch. What some anglers seem to forget, however, is that hot-spots, especially in rivers, can, and do, lose their reliability. For example, fishing pressure may cause the fish to leave a favourite haunt. Furthermore, the bed of a river is constantly changing due to the effects of floods, etc, so what was a comfortable and/or rich feeding ground for the fish may change for the worse. And, of course, there are times when the reverse is true. The reasons for fish to be in a given place varies from day to day, and sometimes even from minute to minute. Bear in mind that it only takes a very short time for a fish to swim from one side of the river to the other.

I have always been intrigued by the idea of 'reading water'. Only a few anglers seem really skilled in this most refined facet of river fishing, which is perfectly understandable. You are dealing with a constantly changing medium which requires a certain understanding of the make-up and condition of the water – temperature, speed of flow, opacity, oxygen content, and a hundred-and-one other things that combine to make big-fish lies.

Although the location of big fish, even when you can't actually see them, is all important, it is not as difficult as it would at first appear. Although the heavier flow, which invariably accompanies turbid conditions, makes the majority of their usual refuges most uncomfortable places for the fish to live and feed in, they will not be far away.

Lush streamer-weed that grew so profusely in the summer has been killed by the autumn frosts and washed away, leaving little to deflect and/or slow the torrent that the fish must now contend with. A small depression in the river-bed that afforded comfort in the warmer months is now a 'boiling cauldron' of ever-changing currents. A barbel, say, combating this faster water, continually changing his lie, soon gets tired and searches out more restful water. But he is not going to move further from his summer haunts than he has to.

It follows, of course, that these more desirable fishy residences need not be close to the bank. Indeed, there are as many in midstream as there are close to the bank. In fact, they can occur anywhere in the river. Surface water racing downstream often camouflages much slower moving water nearer the river's bed. Recognising where this is the case calls for close observation.

An example I know looks like this: there is an area of rough 'broken' water immediately followed by smooth oily-looking water. In the case in question there is a large boulder in the river's bed which causes the surface to 'boil'. Downstream of the boulder a depression has been eroded, scoured out by the current. After breaking on the obstruction caused by the boulder, the water drops into this hole, smoothing the surface and giving the observant angler a clue to the fishes' whereabouts. However, the angler must not be misled into believing that the deeper and more comfortable water for the fish is directly below the smooth area on the surface. Undoubtedly, the 'readings' on the surface caused by the contours in the river-bed will be some way further downstream. By how far downstream will depend on the depth and speed of the water. Of course, the greater these are, the higher upstream the cast must be made to allow the terminal tackle to settle in the correct place – that is, the depression.

In such a swim the 'upstream leger' is a well-tried and trusted method. Sometimes, several casts have to be made before the bait is placed correctly in the lie. This is because, more often than not, the speed and power of the current is underestimated and the tackle is carried downstream before it can be held in place by the slower water in the hole. Therefore, if you are in doubt, cast much farther upstream than is strictly necessary and inch the tackle into position. (It is better to do this anyway rather than to frighten the fish by casting a heavy bomb right in among them.) You will know when the terminal tackle is in the correct place by watching your line, which will be at a steeper, more acute angle when the bait is in place. Also, there will be less pressure on the line.

Almost invariably, bites in this sort of swim are of the classic upstream-leger kind – that is, a quick pull will be followed by the line falling slack, giving you plenty of time to hit it. A long sweeping strike must be made, though, to pick up the slack line.

Bridges are noted holding areas. Whatever the season,

fish, and some big ones too, will be in their vicinity. Many bridge swims are obvious, like the ones directly downstream of the pilings. Big barbel, as well as other species, are often located here for diverse reasons. Three of the important ones are: a surfeit of natural food collects on or near the piers, creating a well-stocked larder; the racing water associated with floods is most efficiently deflected by them (as, of course, they are designed to); and, because these swims are difficult to fish effectively, the fish feel secure from their worst enemy – man.

Sometimes, and nearly always in winter, it is often almost impossible to present a bait naturally in such a swim, but it is well worth trying on every visit, because the day it can be done is likely to be a red-letter occasion. It is impossible, even for the most well-trained eye, to notice every alteration in the prevailing conditions. A change which determines whether a fish will feed or not, or whether the bait can be presented naturally enough to fool the fish or not, can be extremely subtle. My own maxim these days is to try anyway. Plainly, it is preferable to be wrong if the fish won't have it rather than vice-versa. The foregoing observation, of course, is true not just of bridge swims and does not discount other swims that are awkward to fish.

A bridge swim which is not quite so obvious can sometimes be found immediately upstream of the bridge buttress. A deep hole, often spacious enough to accommodate several big fish, is not an unusual occurrence here. Indeed, on a stretch of river in which the majority of my barbelling used to be done, one of the most consistent swims is just as the one described.

Bridges span rivers where they will be the least expensive to build. This usually means where the river is narrow and, as narrow more often than not signifies deep water, it follows that it means big fish too. In the search for bigger-than-average river fish, water in the immediate vicinity of bridges must not be discounted lightly.

On the rivers I fish, slack-water swims are probably the most consistent in terms of numbers of fish caught, especially in the wintertime. There is good reason for this. When the fish are forced from their more usual haunts by increased flow, they obviously seek out more restful water. That is not the only criteria at work, of course – for example, food must be available as well.

● *Peter Frost is watched by Bill Keal as he deals with a big pike (Alec Lewis)*

Many and varied are these slack-water swims (although areas containing dead slack or eddying water are not very reliable). Some are deep, while others have barely enough depth to cover the fishes' backs. Some contain many fish, sometimes even of differing species; others house a solitary loner, like a swim I used to know; seven times in one winter the same big barbel was extracted from it by my friends and myself, and I don't doubt that this same fish was caught from that same slack by other anglers as well.

The position of slack-water swims varies with the amount of water the river is carrying, but in the main they are in the same area summer and winter alike. It is true to say, though, that some slacks disappear with the coming of the spates, but on the other hand, many more come into existence. What cannot be guaranteed is that they will be in the identical places year after year. So, it's a case of looking time and again.

When I used to fish the famed Hampshire Avon's Royalty Fishery regularly in the wintertime, it was noted that barbel especially were caught in different areas of the same slacks, depending on the height of the water. In the Railway Slack, the tendency was for the fish to move further upstream; conversely, in Fiddlers they would be caught lower downstream. This is a generalisation, of course, but what must be remembered is that in high water, more often than not, shoals of fish will be broken down into smaller groups. Therefore, the fish can be found in more than one area in a known swim and the consistently successful big-fish angler finds where the fish are rather than trying to bring the fish to him.

Keeping in mind the second of Dick Walker's 'five essentials', it is of no use finding the fish if you then frighten them away. Remembering this and realising that high water and strong currents can drive many big fish into the margins, it is important to keep well back from the water's edge as much as possible. You won't strain your eyes when searching for swims by staying no nearer than about 10ft of the the river's edge. What is more, it is safer, too: while your attention is concentrated on scanning the river for possible holding areas, you are not likely to plunge into freezing water, right over your waders.

Big-fish holding areas in high and/or coloured water can be found fairly easily by keeping your eyes firmly open. Deeper, hence slower, moving water betrays its presence by many clues, either single or collective. The following are some of the more usual: smooth, 'oily' surface; a generally darker area of water; where the current slows; where the river narrows, especially if the pace of the current shows a slight or no increase in speed. A naturally steeper bank, very likely undercut, often denotes that deeper water exists at its base as well.

Specimen-sized fish often congregate where tributaries join the main river to take advantage of the deeper water that exists there. The sidestream brings down food for the fish to enjoy, without expending too much energy to harvest it. Also, particularly at times of spates, the stream rushing into the river diverts the main flow, forming an area of comparative comfort for the fish. This area of slower water is more often located downstream of the tributary mouth, but sometimes a swim is formed upstream, albeit on a generally smaller scale.

Many authorities recommend raft-type swims for chub and I agree with the general principle. However, I have not found this sort of swim very reliable in producing very big chub – say, over 5½lb. For fish of this stamp one must look at the river a little bit harder. More reliable is a swim in open water that is undisturbed by bankside activity. A swim which requires a difficult cast, a long walk, or anything that deters other anglers is always worth investigating. It is my experience that very big chub do not like rough or 'boiling' water; an even, steady flow is much more suitable.

Another winning area is where slower water joins a faster current, forming a crease. So, too, are the margins of weir-pools, especially if they are surrounded and overhung with trees or bushes, making casting tricky or difficult. It seems that some chub anglers are too worried about getting hung up and avoid such areas, passing up the chance of a specimen chub in the process. Big chub can turn up in the most unexpected places and, once caught and returned, are rarely seen again. This fact is unlike the case for other species. Big barbel, for example, are often caught over and over again, often suggesting that there are more of them about than there actually are. Don't discount a likely-looking chub swim because it hasn't produced a successful catch in the past. Like most other anglers, I used to discount such areas, but not since an incident opened my eyes.

I had spent a day fishing the Dorset Stour, together with Keith Griffin and my son, Tony. Despite promising chub conditions, it proved a gruelling exercise. At dusk, Tony and I were anxious to exchange the cold riverbank for a warm restaurant, and we went to find Keith. We discovered him, concentrating deeply, because he was getting some small bites. Keith asked us to give him another half-hour to try to catch one. So Tony and I went to fish a spot that although it looked like a banker chub swim, it had failed to produce, not only that day but several times in the past as well. On the first cast I missed a very hard pull, but made no mistake on the second. As it came over the net, Tony said, 'Blimey! How big do you want this one to be, Dad?' It turned out to be exactly 6lb – my heaviest chub of that particular season.

Here, I would like to make an important point. Even though you may be out on the bank in search of one species, you can observe and note the location of specimens of a different species. I have lost count of the times that this has happened to me, and it is considered as a valuable bonus. The location of big pike is an obvious example.

Anyone who has spent any length of time wandering the rivers' banks cannot have failed to frighten a pike from a position close to the river's edge. Furthermore, even the most unobservant angler cannot fail to notice the large bow-wave a frightened pike makes as it bolts across the river. And, often, the more impressive the bow-wave that is created, the larger the pike. Despite consciously trying to avoid any unnecessary noise on the riverbank, such as making heavy foot-falls, dropping tackle, speaking loudly, etc, I still scare far too many fish. Obviously, once you have scared a large pike you can't unscare it, but this does not prevent you from taking some advantage of the situation. You now know the whereabouts of it, knowledge that you can put to good use on another occasion. But this time you will advance with much more circumspection; now you know where it lives, you won't want to frighten it again – not if you want to catch it that day, that is.

Not all large pike will be found close to the banks, though, and just as many will be found further out. Close to the branches of fallen trees, weed-beds, or anything else that deflects the flow, are obvious places to try.

Bushes which overhang and droop, through which the water filters and forms rafts of flotsam, is another good place for large pike (perhaps that is the reason why very large chub avoid such areas!). One of Britain's most successful river-pike anglers, Bob Mousley, once told me that he doesn't catch many pike in water less than 2ft deep or more than 8ft deep. It would be a brave

● *'Blimey! How big do you want this one to be, Dad?'*
Answer – exactly 6lb!

or unwise man who ignores advice from someone of Bob's extensive experience.

Pike will not be found very far from an abundant supply of fodder fish. Therefore, a stretch that consistently produces large bags of suitable sized fish – for example, dace, roach, chub, up to around 1lb, etc – is well worth investigation. If there are not enough matches or pleasure catches to go on, you will have little alternative but to do the spade-work yourself.

A clean, sandy or gravelly bottom, with no trace of mud, is the place to start your search for roach. They also are very fond of the slower, even-paced water adjacent to a swifter stream. They dislike swift water, I suppose, because of their bulky shape.

J. W. Martin, who spent forty years roach fishing, wrote about locating river roach thus:

They like the slow, lazy curls under bushes, the quiet lay-byes or corners away from the main stream; swims that flow at not more than two miles an hour, or in the curls, eddies and dimples in the vicinity of a weir, or in the immediate neighbourhood of an old wooden bridge, and sometimes in the shallows of a mill tail.

The old Trent Otter certainly knew what he was talking about and, in my opinion, these remain the principle places to look for roach in a swiftly flowing river.

Gerry Swanton, who has caught more than 300 roach of 2lb and over, said in a recent edition of the *Angler's Mail,*

Chalk streams do not produce large numbers of big roach during the summer, so most of my river roach fishing is done from November onwards. Most of my

fish come from slow, deep glides or along the crease of an eddy. The inside of bends is a favourite location . . . I love floods as the fish can be driven to within three feet of the bank, and laying-on in these conditions can be very rewarding.

Although a considerable amount of observation and experience is required to become a proficient 'reader of rivers', it is not a difficult task. And as American writer, Gene Hill, puts it,

. . . but this doesn't detract from my belief that reading water is about the highest level of accomplishment a fisherman can aspire to. It requires a nice blend of science and wishful thinking and an ability to marry what you can't see and what you can.

All this trouble is well worth the effort, for it pays for itself over and over again by putting more fish and bigger fish on the bank. Without wishing to boast, during the 1989–90 winter, I photographed more than ten chub over 5lb each and at least seven different double-figure barbel, in addition to specimen roach and pike. And, during that winter the rains did not arrive in earnest until well after Christmas.

4
Tackle

It is extremely difficult for anyone who has taken up fishing in the past few years to realise how radically specialised tackle has changed. Just twenty-five years ago, apart from a few rods, there was precious little in the way of purposely designed tackle. Necessary items that were considered not viable, for any reason, by the tackle barons had to be modified or home-made, or you went without. Initially, it was Richard Walker who did more than anyone to rectify this situation, by designing and making sound tackle and then demonstrating that it worked satisfactorily and successfully. However, as a whole, the tackle trade was slow to catch on.

To be fair, the major tackle manufacturers could not justify the costs of design and development at a time when the potential market was so tiny compared to the size of the market today. It was left to the smaller, more progressive tackle businesses to exploit the gap. Front-runners among these companies were B. James & Son of Ealing, West London, who produced, among other equipment, specialist rods and landing-nets based on Dick Walker's designs.

But the situation really improved when far-seeing individuals such as Peter Drennan produced a wide range of well-designed tackle, of good quality, in quantity and at reasonable prices. Eventually, this policy resulted in the happy situation that all anglers take for granted today, in which just about every conceivable taste is catered for with a wide range of tackle readily available.

This chapter will cover the latest tackle that I have been using in my attempts to extract big fish, excepting pike from rivers (see Chapter 8).

Rods

The modern carbon-fibre rod, like those made from boron, Kevlar and other various composites, casts further and more accurately, picks up line quicker, and is essentially stronger, lighter and more durable than anything that has preceded it. The adaptability of this material however, does not guarantee that one single design will answer all situations and circumstances – far from it. Therefore, unless you are rich enough to afford a rod to suit every purpose or contingency, a compromise has to be reached. But this need not mean that you have to sacrifice efficiency. Any new rod should be assessed carefully, making sure that it is adequate for the job in hand and, wherever possible, ensuring that it will handle other situations. Versatility is the key word.

Leger rods

The latest addition to my armoury is a weapon from the Drennan Company called the Bomb Rod, and a more delightful rod is almost impossible to imagine. It is designed primarily for the specialist matchman, as the perfect tool for light leger work down the inside line. The sensible length of 10ft 6in also makes it ideal for general leger work on smallish, and not too powerful, rivers and streams. After the weed has died down, the Bomb Rod is currently my first legering choice on the Kennet and, if the pace of the current is sufficiently sedate, the Dorset Stour. The Bomb Rod's twin-top joints have ultra-fine built-in quiver-tips of just ½oz and ¾oz test curve. Despite this lightness, they will handle a wide range of bomb weights (⅛oz to 1oz being quoted), as well as light feeders and link-legers.

Bite detection is absolutely superb with the Bomb Rod and the size and duration of bites is actually increased and prolonged due to the extremely low tip resistance. This is an absolutely vital consideration when touch legering and/or when tentative bites are expected – in my experience, virtually 100 per cent of the time. The Fuji silicon carbide-lined rings (SIC), fitted throughout, are robust, virtually wearproof and ensure that especially fine lines are safeguarded from premature damage due to the twin evils of heat and friction. The makers recommend ideal reel lines of 1½–3lb, but I have gone as high as 6lb bs with no ill-effects.

Of course, the fineness of the rod, especially the tips, must be respected – for example, you wouldn't use it where overhanging branches, etc, impede the strike. Nevertheless, its 1½lb power curve ensures that it still has good reserves of power in the lower sections and will therefore handle and land big fish. A few days ago, on a carrier of the Hampshire Avon, the Bomb Rod accounted for an accidentally caught large and hard-fighting common carp, in addition to big roach and chub.

For legering more powerful streams, I now choose another Drennan rod – the 13ft Feeder. Built in IM8 carbon, the 13ft Feeder is light in weight, beautifully balanced and, therefore, easy to handle. And, being of low diameter, it is less affected by wind, which makes it ideal in those achingly yearned for, wet-and-windy winter conditions that are seemingly so beloved of big barbel – and me! Of course, this does not mean that the 13ft Feeder is unsuitable for summer use – nothing could be further from the truth: Bob James uses a pair of them, summer and winter, in his stunningly prolific quest for enormous river fish. The only modification has been the addition of a small, yet powerful, betalight, to aid after-dark bite detection.

The Feeder is designed primarily for distance river fishing, will cast weights up to and including 2oz, and the extra length and extra power make long-distance casting and good line control very easy. It comes equipped with two quiver-tips: one of glass-fibre, with a 2oz test curve for soft responsive bite detection; the other is a 2½oz test curve carbon-fibre with faster, more springy recovery for 'drop-back' bites. The latter type is very useful in an upstream legering situation. Versatility is further increased because the 13ft Feeder will also accommodate the wider range of quiver-tips used in the Drennan Light, Medium and Big Feeder rods. Recommended reel lines are 3–6lb bs.

Float rod

When float fishing for long periods, especially at long range, it is difficult to imagine that anything could be more perfect than the latest 12ft IM8 Super Crystalight. This is another superlative tool produced by the Drennan Company.

Although this IM8 Crystalight is both thinner and approximately 1oz lighter than the IM6 model, in the butt and middle it has slightly greater reserves of power. This pushes the action forward towards the tip and makes it a better rod for playing bigger fish. While it is faster and more crisp than the mellow IM6 Crystalight, the tip retains all its lightness and delicacy and allows hook-links down to 6oz to be used. It is equipped with a 20in cork handle and Fuji full-bridge SIC rings. The recommended line strengths are 1.7–2.6lb for reel lines, and 6oz–11lb 8oz for hook-links.

Reels

It seems to me that nowadays river anglers increasingly are using centre-pin reels, but, frankly, I can't see the need. I don't deny the undoubted aesthetic qualities of the centre-pin in skilled hands; however, total efficiency is my aim, so in my view, only reels of the fixed-spool type are really worth considering. Nevertheless, if it pleases you to fish with a centre-pin, do so. There still is more to fishing than just catching fish. And I have used a variety of reels down the years, including centre-pins, but there are three models, all fixed spool, that stand out from the rest.

There was a time when all big-fish men relied on Mitchell reels and, even today, you could do worse than to use a Mitchell 300 or 410. But the unreliable line-roller, together with a clutch that needs continual adjustment, and the fact that it is prone to tangles, meant that I had to look elsewhere.

Superb engineering is the hallmark of ABU's early Cardinal 54 model. The line-roller and clutch is superb and I would still be using mine today if another reel with a unique feature had not been introduced – Shimano's Bait-runner. The Bait-runner feature is a great boon in some styles of river fishing, notably for barbel. It allows a fish to take line freely without leaving the bail-arm open. By moving the bait-runner lever forward, the reel's gearing is disengaged. However, the tension provided can still be adjusted and pre-set to overcome, for example, the power of the current. To return to 'conventional' mode, you simply turn the reel handle forward.

The latest Shimano Aero Bait-runners are made in several sizes; the smallest, the 3500, are ideal for river fishing. At the time of writing, my bait-runners have done one full season's hard work without any problems of unreliability, and a tangle is rare. My only complaint is that the anti-reverse lever, situated under the reel, is fiddly to operate, although the standard handles have been changed for the smaller, neater ones from the 2000 GTM Aero model.

The 2000 GTM Aero is a little jewel. Ron Chant and Bob James use them 'bait-runner fashion' when fishing for barbel with the rod(s) in their rests. To do this, the 'fighting-drag' lever is set to allow the spool to just not revolve to the pull of the current. It is then adjusted to the required tension once the fish is hooked. Ron and Bob have caught many hard-fighting fish using the 2000 GTM Aero this way, but, be warned, this model was not intended for such use.

Lines and Hooks

The most important items of tackle, whatever the quarry, are lines and hooks. A skilful angler, if pressed, can successfully cope with the liabilities imposed by poor rods and reels, but he must employ the very best lines and hooks if he is to enjoy consistent success.

There are certain properties that affect monofilament lines. The six most important are described below:

1 *Knot strength*   This is generally lower on matt lines and highest on a hard glossy line. Different types of knot suit different types of line, but the best knots like the Grinner and the Overturn Whipping knot are good in all types of line (see Figs 2 and 3).

2 *Abrasion resistance*   Often related to knot strength, you don't want a line that gets roughed up too easily or which loses a high proportion of its strength from the slightest damage.

3 *Optimum stretch*   A nice degree of elasticity is required; too much can prove a handicap, particularly when distance fishing, and too little is a recipe for sudden breakages.

4 *Shelf life*   Inexplicably, some lines do not keep well, deteriorating very quickly and losing much of their strength after just a few months. If you are about to reuse a line after a gap of two or three months, it is always best to pull test it properly on a spring balance. (Don't use your best fish-weighing balance to do this, because a snapping line lets the balance suddenly jolt back, thus ruining the accuracy of the instrument in the process.)

5 *Suppleness*   This helps both distance and accuracy when casting, avoids tangles and even aids bait presentation. Some perfectly good lines seem springy at first but just need gently stretching before fishing. Others have a tendency to coil and should be avoided.

6 *Strength*   This is the most important property; however, it is the breaking strain × the diameter ratio which is the key. Some lines are not the diameter they claim to be and the situation is further confused by the English tradition of under-rating the breaking strain.

Of the many monofilament lines available, my own choice for most legering situations is Drennan's Specimen Plus. This brand has good knot strength, is abrasion resistant, not too stretchy, supple, has a satin matt surface of pleasing colour (copper brown) and, above all these considerations, is very reliable, being accurately and consistently rated. Available on 100m or 600m bulk spools, this tough and highly durable line is fast sinking, super strong and very economical; it is therefore, ideal for big-fish angling.

Further excellent monofilaments for legering are Maxima, Racine, and, according to Roger Smith, Brent is cheap and reliable. I have included these other makes because a line that suits me may not suit you, or vice versa. There is, however, another line that Kevin Clifford comes close to enthusing about, which is Berkeley's Big Game line. In *Big Fish World* magazine Kevin described it like this:

Right then, here's something special. Terry Eustace is now the British distributor for Berkeley Big Game line and there is no doubt in my mind that it has some exceptional qualities. The line is particularly abrasion resistant and I recently went over to Birmingham where Terry gave me a demonstration. The results of this can be seen in Terry's advert, but being impressed yet something of a sceptic by nature, I thought I'd carry out a few tests of my own. You never know, Terry might have had the other line kicking around from the days when he actually went carp fishing.

My own tests, using a similar procedure to Terry's, which I accept are only a rough guide, clearly demonstrate the abrasion-resistant qualities of Berkeley Big Game line. The other line I used for comparison was not the same one used in Terry's tests. I used a line which I have been fishing with for the last couple of seasons and which has given no cause for complaint. A weight was fastened to the

● Fig 2 *The grinner knot: a reliable knot for eyed hooks and swivels*

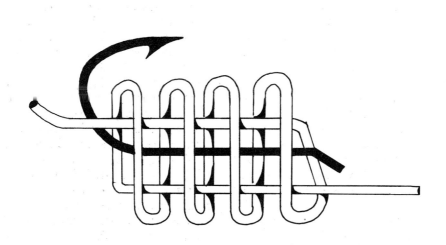

● Fig 3 *The overturn whipping knot: one of the best knots for spade-end hooks*

end of the line and this was pulled over the edge of a piece of glass for a measured distance. These are the results:

No of Lifts Before the Line Broke

	Very Popular 12lb Line	12lb Berkeley Big Game Line
1st test	14	24
2nd test	7	31
3rd test	13	44
4th test	5	37
5th test	17	8
6th test	13	28

Interestingly, I also tried the same test using a couple of well-known braids in 12lb breaking strain. They could only manage two or three lifts before breaking, and this really does bring into question their claimed abrasion-resistant qualities as far as I am concerned.

When Terry first showed me a spool of the Berkeley Big Game line I was deterred by its colour, or lack of it, because it is white, but try this simple test. Tie a length of Berkeley, along with a couple of lengths of line which are coloured dark brown or green (which most lines are nowadays), to a lead and let it settle on, or near, the bed of the lake. You will discover that the Berkeley is almost invisible compared to the darker coloured lines, which stand out like a sore thumb.

If you are intending to fish any of those lakes in France, which are full of snags and boulders, then the Berkeley Big Game line is an absolute must. It will definitely reduce losses. I am using the 12lb for barbel fishing near some snags, where I have lost a fair percentage of the fish I have hooked in the past. I am full of confidence that the Berkeley Big Game line will cut those losses down considerably. Finally, Terry has discovered that the Berkeley Big Game line does not perform well when the blood knot is used, which, although I have used it a great deal myself, I acknowledge is not a particularly good knot.

The Berkeley Big Game line is available in breaking strains of 10lb, 12lb, 15lb and 20lb, in green as well as in the original white. All heavier breaking strains are available in white only.

Where or when it is essential to use the finest line available, you can do no better than the Drennan Double Strength (which isn't pre-stretched). However, you must realise that this is completely different from ordinary monofilament and learn to choose your Double Strength by diameter and not by breaking strain. There are three very important reasons for this:

1 Line damage has a far greater effect on thin line than on thick line of the same breaking strain.
2 Being thinner, 5lb Double Strength at .007in will be far less forgiving than 5lb standard at .009in when a bad knot is tied.
3 Lines are traditionally under-rated, so the standard 5lb line will probably break at about 6lb, whereas Double Strength line is accurately rated and will normally break at the stated breaking strain.

Therefore, instead of your old 5lb line, use 10lb Double Strength which is still the same .009in diameter, or if you want to fish both finer and stronger, use 7lb Double Strength at .008in.

Another unique feature of the Double Strength line is that it is a resin-bonded and impregnated co-polymide material – that is, it is not nylon. This gives it its surface sheen and minimises water absorption. All nylon monofilaments are hygroscopic and many lose up to 20 per cent of their dry breaking strain after immersion in water for just a couple of hours. Drennan Double Strength retains a remarkable 94 per cent of its dry strength even after seven hours immersion.

When it comes to bomb and feeder fishing, the enormous reduction in diameters means that you can drastically reduce the amount of weight required to hold bottom. A 4lb standard monofilament is .008in, whereas 4lb Double Strength is .006in; that two thousandth of an inch difference over 30yd of line adds up to an incredible 2sq in of extra surface area – that is, the water resistance on Double Strength is 25 per cent less.

It must be remembered, however, that, like all other small diameter lines, the slightest nick will seriously affect its strength, and I find that it is also likely to break when subjected to sudden shocks. Furthermore, if the tackle is unduly strained, such as pulling out of weed, etc, any line can lose a proportion of its inherent strength. The moral then is clear – when using Double Strength, be constantly alert for any damage and employ the softest rods suitable for the job in hand. To reduce the chance of breakage still further, where possible it is advisable to make just the hook-link from Double Strength. Then the elasticity of the reel line, say

Specimen Plus, will, to some extent, absorb most shocks, particularly if the hook-link is of a higher breaking strain than the reel line. As mentioned earlier, fishing with Double Strength this way means that you get the best of both worlds – a stronger, yet finer and more supple hook-link.

Some authorities recommend the joining of Double Strength to ordinary monofilament by means of a double grinner knot, but I don't do it this way. I feel that this method could result in the harder line cutting through the softer one, particularly during an extended battle with a big fish. Admittedly, the risk is probably small, but I feel happier using a swivel or small Drennan ring at the junction between the lines. And, no matter how small, why take any unnecessary risk?

Because braided line is prone to tangling after continually twisting in rapidly running water, I rarely use it when fishing rivers; furthermore, there seems to be no necessity to use it.

Many, if not most, specialist anglers have come to rely on Drennan hooks, and Peter Drennan explains why:

In recent seasons there has been a complete hook revolution with the latest Japanese manufacturing techniques providing British anglers with a new range of hooks of unparalleled strength and sharpness. Not only has their high carbon steel proved totally superior to the standard European wire, but the Japanese have successfully designed and built machinery to manufacture to new standards of accuracy. By this method hooks are made with ground and chemically etched needle-points which are sharper and more durable than the European cut point. Of equal benefit, much smaller low-profile barbs can also be produced.

Drennan Fishing Tackle working in close association with the manufacturers have now developed a range of hooks perfectly suited to the needs of UK anglers. By then imposing our own strict inspection and quality control on top of the truly excellent standards set by our suppliers, we can provide what are simply the best and most reliable hooks available.

Needless to say, I use several Drennan types, including the popular Carbon Specimen and Super Specialist patterns, but it is the newer patterns that especially excite me. One such is the Star Point hook which in many ways is revolutionary. Because of its unique anti-eject bend, the point is angled, more or less, in line with the eye. This feature encouraged the belief that the Star Point would behave in much the same way as the renowned bent-hook, and practice bore out the theory. In fact, the Star Point works even better and has the advantage of inflicting no discernible damage to the fish.

There is no doubt that the Star Point's increased effectiveness is due in no small part to the saving in weight, when compared to a similar gaped bent-hook, which improves bait presentation. Also, its much easier penetration must have considerable bearing on its effectiveness, too. The point of the Star Point is designed on the principle that is well understood by the makers of swords and bayonets, etc: the micro-engineered flutes hold the flesh apart, thereby reducing friction and so aiding penetration. Therefore, this, coupled with a chemically etched needle-point, means that the Star Point needs much less force to achieve penetration than an equivalent-sized hook with a conventional point.

Kamatsu were the first high-tech hooks I encountered. Their chemically contrived sharpness soon became famous and everyone seemed to be using them. Nowadays, they have changed their name to Kamasan and although the name is different, the quality remains the same – first class. I invariably use pattern B980.

Other reliable hooks are available, among which are Partridge's Jack Hilton Carp, Mustad's 34021, and several models from Au Lion d'Or. The latter company's 1535 is very strong and the 1540 pattern is stronger still; both have spade-ends, the type I prefer. For hooks which are similar in all other respects, a spade-end will not weigh as much as its eyed counterpart, which must improve presentation significantly.

Spade-ends have the undeserved reputation of cutting through line. In more than thirty years of using hooks of this type, never once have I had the remotest suspicion that a fish has been lost because the spade-end cut the line. Perhaps I have just been lucky or, more likely, have taken the trouble to learn how to tie knots correctly.

To avoid any chance of rust attacking hooks, smear the inside of the plastic box with a neutral, odourless grease like Vaseline. This has the added advantage that if the opened box is dropped, at least some of the hooks will remain stuck inside.

There was a time, not long ago, when I would never

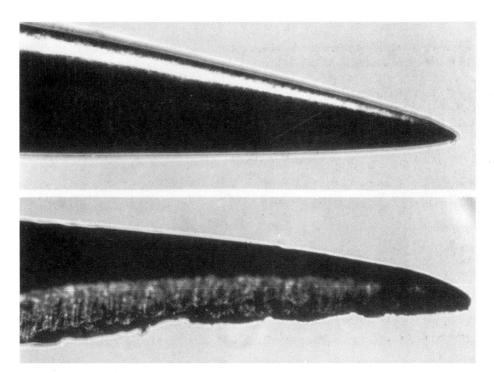

have considered using ready-tied hooks. However, the recent vast improvement in quality, and my rapidly failing eyesight, made me think again. Not that I could ever tie small hooks to fine hook-links very neatly, and certainly not to the standard of Drennan ready-tied hooks.

When feeder fishing, my choice is either a size 14 Carbon Feeder or a size 16 Carbon Chub, from the hook to nylon range. I always use the former if there is any likelihood of barbel. This pattern's combination of a wide gape and curved point will reduce the number of missed bites for, when it is used in conjunction with heavy feeders, many more fish will hook themselves. The latter hook is perfect for that most difficult situation of fine line and delicate single maggot presentation, which produces more than the odd big chub.

With the ever-increasing need for improved presentation, particularly when float fishing, more and more anglers are looking at not only the quality of the hook, but also to the line on to which they are tied. Obviously, the finer the line, the better the presentation, something which tackle innovator Peter Drennan realised when he released the Double Strength line. The Drennan range of hooks are, as we have seen, superb, and it seems a logical progression to marry the two together and so provide a pre-tied, good quality hook to good quality

● *a) The ground and chemically etched needle-point of a Drennan Carbon Match hook size 16, magnified 100 times*
b) The cut point of a similar match hook produced by the latest European technology, also magnified 100 times

line. To fulfil this need, Drennan now offer hooks ready tied to Double Strength.

Four popular patterns are available, all with a proven track-record. *Coarse Fisherman* magazine editor, Simon Roff, an experienced and successful match angler, had this to say about Drennan hooks tied to Double Strength:

The line diameter/strengths have been married to the sizes and styles of hooks correctly (obviously by a match angler) and most patterns have a choice of line strength in each size, giving the angler greater choice. The actual whipping can't be faulted, it's certainly a match for any self-tied hooks and all are supplied with 22in of line, enabling the angler to choose how long he wants his hook length.

I cannot over-emphasise the importance of testing every hook before use. You cannot be too particular or too careful when it comes to hooks and/or lines, not discounting every other part of your tackle. Reliable knots are illustrated in Figs 2 and 3.

Leger Stops

These tiny yet vitally important items need to be readily adjustable, quite capable of standing severe shock without slipping and must not cut into the line. If the leger stop was to slip, the only sure result would be a frayed line which could easily result in a lost fish. A simple yet effective leger stop which satisfies every criterion can be made easily. A ½in long piece of soft wood (a pared-down matchstick) is plugged into two ¼in long pieces of previously cleaned out Biro tube; when wet, the wood swells, ensuring a very tight fit. For absolute security, the line is turned around the wooden peg two or three times.

An excellent leger stop which is available over the counter, for those who haven't the time or inclination to make their own, is a new Drennan design. This consists of the conventional principle of a small piece of plastic

● Fig 4 *A typical link-leger set-up, showing an 'exploded' view of a home-made leger-stop*

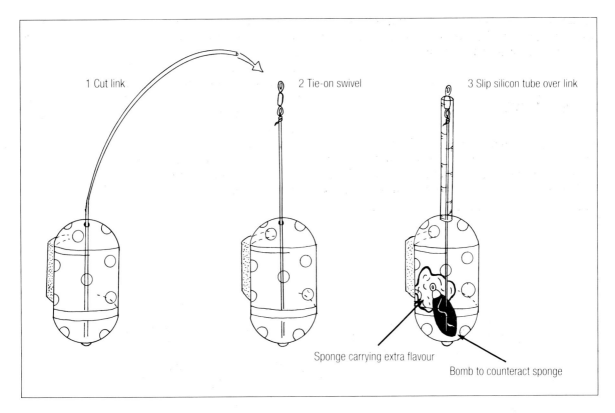

1 Cut link   2 Tie-on swivel   3 Slip silicon tube over link

Sponge carrying extra flavour

Bomb to counteract sponge

● Fig 5 *Feeder modification to prevent tangles*

tube plugged by a plastic peg. The peg, however, is a clever design, which has the line passing through it, which ensures that the stop is centred about the line (instead of being biased to one side, as in other designs). This is yet another improvement in presentation.

Whatever type of leger stop you use, a small piece of silicon-rubber tube, on the line above it, will help it to absorb shocks without slipping.

Swim-feeders

There are so many well-designed and well-manufactured swim-feeders available these days that it would be impossible to cover them all. Suffice it to say that I generally use one of two Drennan patterns when river fishing. For maggots, I use an Oval Block-end, which comes in three sizes – ¾oz, 1½oz and 2oz. And for cereal baits, etc, I use the Stainless Cage-feeders, of which four sizes are available.

Invariably, in my case, the feeder is used on a sliding link, in place of a bomb. Used thus, it has a nasty habit

of tangling. This annoyance can be considerably reduced by a simple modification. Just cover the link with a suitable length of silicon-rubber tubing (the tube is kept in position by locating it on the swivel – see Fig 5).

On very hot days, maggots are at their liveliest and escape the block-end almost before it is cast. To prevent this, at least some of the holes need blocking up. Electricians' black adhesive tape wrapped around the feeder is a simple yet effective method, but PVA tape, held in position by a couple of rubber-bands, though a bit more fiddly, is better. It ensures that the feeder deposits all its contents in the swim. The disadvantage with the PVA method is that it has to be repeated for each cast, whereas the adhesive tape can be left in position indefinitely.

Recently, I have been experimenting by adding a piece of sponge soaked in synthetic flavour, or Richworth Feed-inducing Rig Tablets, to my block-end feeders. This tactic ensures that there is a good flavour leak-off and scented trail to draw the fish to the swim, without the risk of overfeeding. To counteract the buoyancy of the sponge, simply pop a small non-toxic bomb in the feeder (see Fig 5).

Leger Weights

Relatively recent legislation bars anglers from using lead weights in sizes No 8 to 1oz inclusive; but this restriction should prove no disadvantage as excellent alternatives are now available. Some non-toxic weights, though, have an unsatisfactory shine which disappears with wear and tear. However, soaking in vinegar overnight will remove the shine. Then all they need is a swill under the cold-water tap before they are placed in your tackle-box.

The Interchangeable Link Legers from Drennan need no such treatment and they have the added advantage that the supplied link may be extended by stretching, providing versatile presentation. The link-to-bomb connection is threaded, enabling the weights to be interchanged without breaking down the tackle. The Interchangeable Link Legers come on a handy card in five different weights. Since discovering these, I use them whenever possible.

Landing-nets

It really is a matter of personal preference whether you use a round or triangular-shaped landing-net; my choice is the triangular type.

To obtain the features I consider necessary in a landing-net – light weight coupled with strength and with no loose pieces to lose – I designed and made my own net. It has 36in hollow glass arms which spring into a strong spreader (machined from Tufnol), which is permanently fixed to the extending glass handle. The extending handle is an important point: high banks are a feature of many rivers and they become slippery and hence dangerous when wet. So, unless you want to lose the chance of landing that monster, or are looking to take an early bath, or both, your landing-net must be equipped with a long handle, and the extending type is best.

Also important is the mesh. It is best to use one of the knotless micromeshes which are kinder to fish because they do not remove the scales from roach, etc, and neither do they split fins and/or tails, nor tangle barbels' dorsal fins, as coarse, knotted meshes were always prone to do. Indeed, the use of knotted meshes and nets is now illegal.

Keep-nets, Keep-sacks and Tunnels

Under no circumstances should a keep-net be used for retaining barbel, as they are quite unsuitable for this purpose. They are also now unnecessary – keep-sacks and tunnels are ideal for retaining barbel, not discounting other fish, and excellent examples are available from all good tackle outlets. You must not keep more than one fish at a time in either a keep-sack or a tunnel.

It may be prudent to quote here the latest National Rivers Authority's regulations regarding fish retainers:

A   No person shall use a keep-net having a depth of less than 1.5m (5ft) when fully extended or having hoops of less than 35cm (13¾in) external diameter or if rectangular of less than 35cm (13¾in) by 30cm (12in). The keep-net shall be constructed from a knotless material and the mesh shall not be smaller than 6mm (¼in) internal circumference or approximately 2mm (.1in) internal diameter.

B   Keep-sacks and keep-tunnels may be used for the retention of fish, provided that not more than one fish is retained in a keep-sack or keep tunnel at any one time. For the purpose of this byelaw:

   (i)   a keep-sack shall have a minimum size of 90cm (35½in) by 120cm (47¼in), be constructed of dark coloured, soft, non-abrasive, permeable fabric with rounded corners;
   (ii) a keep-tunnel shall be constructed of a dark coloured, soft, non-abrasive, permeable fabric, supported by a rigid frame, incorporating knotless mesh at one or both ends. The length of any fish retained shall not exceed the length of the keep-tunnel.

5
Bait

It has been said that bait is not the most important aspect in the quest for big fish and, in some circumstances, this may very well be true. But in other cases, the use of the correct bait is absolutely essential for success. How to determine when the use of a particular bait is necessary is the crux of the matter, and only experience will help to determine the answer. Having said that, the acute problem, where big river fish are concerned, is not to find a bait that they will accept, but to discover a bait that is impervious to the attentions of smaller or unwanted fish, such as those slimy abominations, bootlace eels.

Eels are undoubtedly the big-fish angler's number one enemy, especially when fishing rivers. Well known is the fact eels greedily feed on anything meaty, such as worms, maggots, casters, fish (whole or in pieces) or luncheon-meat. What is less well known about eels is that once the sun has gone down, they will eat almost anything. The after-dark fisherman's sanity can sometimes be preserved, however, by using seed-baits. Most of these, with the notable exception of sweetcorn, provide a degree of protection from eels. Also, you might just avoid their unwanted nocturnal attentions by using a big hard hook-bait. But it will have to be very big and very hard. Furthermore, it is worth remembering that eels feed frequently in winter.

Almost as big a nuisance, and just as frustrating, are immature chub – so much so, that one of my friends lists big chub as his favourite river fish and small chub as his least favourite fish. Small chub cannot be avoided by using a big hard bait. The mouth of a 2lb chub is big enough to engulf a golf-ball-sized bait and its throat-teeth are powerful enough to masticate almost anything. Anyone who has seen what a relatively small chub can do to crayfish, complete with shell, will not doubt the veracity of this statement. And beware – don't try to shift a deep-seated hook from a chub's throat with the end of your finger.

If all this makes the problem of nuisance fish sound insurmountable, it is not meant to. Nuisance fish are an intense frustration, but carefully thought out and executed swim preparation gives an excellent chance of catching the stamp of fish we all seek.

Swim Preparation

With each succeeding season I find myself concentrating more and more on preparing swims, by careful feeding, etc, with less time spent actually fishing. This approach has resulted in my catching fewer fish, but the average size has increased almost beyond belief. It was around 1985 when I decided that I had caught enough medium-sized barbel and that I really wanted to set out my stall for bigger fish – that is, fish over 10lb. Fishing the rivers to this approach certainly paid dividends in terms of size. From memory, in the course of that winter, I caught 31 barbel, with no less than 27 of them weighing upwards of 8lb. The heaviest weighed 11lb 2oz, my best at that time. Big chub have also succumbed to this kind of approach. These results are recounted merely to qualify the rewards that careful swim preparation can generate. Anybody who is prepared to put in the effort can do as well, if not better.

The change of approach came with the realisation that it was bad practice to cast into a swim too soon after the initial introduction of feed. Of course, you are likely to get a response on the first cast fishing like this, but most likely it will be from a small or medium-sized fish. Any cautious bigger fish feeding in the area will undoubtedly be upset by the disturbance and are less likely to pick up the bait. It is certainly far more productive, particularly for larger fish, to employ what I call the 'bait-and-wait' approach.

The idea behind the 'bait-and-wait' approach is to develop the swim in several distinct phases, which can be summed up simplistically as follows:

● *Bill Keal hoists ashore a big chub* (Alec Lewis)

1 Introduce bait to attract fish to the swim and entice them to feed.
2 Encourage confidence by doing nothing to disturb them.
3 Larger fish investigate and gain confidence.
4 Large fish invoke 'pecking order' and 'dissuade' lesser fish.
5 Larger fish feed exclusively and confidently.

Ideally, of course, fishing should not commence before · phase 5 is achieved.

In practice, several likely swims are systematically baited, then each is visited in turn. In a perfect world, the water would always be crystal clear, allowing you to see what is going on in the swim. Under such conditions it is relatively straightforward to determine when fishing should begin. More likely, however, the water will be too coloured and/or too deep for observation, or the sun will have set, and in these circumstances you will have to rely more heavily on your instincts. But don't be down-hearted at this statement, look on it positively. By preparing several swims it is unlikely that you will get it wrong in every one of them.

Don't be misled into believing that the bait-and-wait approach is an easy option – it isn't! Like most success-

ful methods it entails considerable thought and effort, not to mention downright hard work, to get the best from it. More likely than not, you will have to visit each prepared swim several times during the session. When you decide on a move, either because no bites are forthcoming, or a small fish is hooked, or for any other reason, more bait should be introduced before moving on. Don't spend too much unproductive time in a prepared swim. If the final phase of feeding has been achieved and a big fish is feeding confidently, it won't take long for it to find your bait. As a general rule, half an hour is more than ample time to wait for a bite. More usually, it comes within a couple of minutes of positioning the hook-bait. (For further details on positioning the hook-bait and free offerings, see Chapter 7.) Unless you are very fortunate indeed, you will have to persist, maybe for some time, before the bait-and-wait approach works. Remember, though, that it is a methodical way of fishing and as such cannot help but ensure that you triumph eventually, so long as you are not easily deterred.

Because it is the best fish attractor I yet know of, cooked hempseed forms the basis of all my pre-baiting on the rivers, whatever the target fish. In fact, it seems that the only species that is not attracted to hemp is eels, which worries me not at all. But, because it is so good, do not let hempseed blind you to the possibilities of other effective fish attractors, which would be a grave mistake.

Small, say ¼in, cubes of luncheon-meat and cheese are good, as are maggots, casters, sweetcorn, maple peas, tares, elderberries, black-eyed beans (boiled in tomato soup), dari-seed, mashed bread, midi boilies, etc – a full list is endless. But, as already stated, whatever is chosen is invariably used in addition to, and in conjunction with, cooked hempseed.

The river's currents will, of course, carry the flavour of the feed downstream and certain additives will make the message even clearer. My favourites include evaporated milk, powdered milk, and, latterly, water-soluble flavours and sweeteners from the Richworth range. The juices that baits have been cooked in or kept in are also ideal for this purpose. For example, when canned sweetcorn is the bait, add the juice from the can to any ground-bait used to carry its scent downstream. Similarly, use water in which hemp, or any other seed, has been cooked for the same purpose.

Once big fish are attracted into the swim to feed, it is desirable to keep them there for as long as possible. The following three tips may help. First, don't introduce large baits that may soon satiate their appetites. Secondly, when possible – that is, when or where eels are not too much of a problem – use at least some maggots; these will burrow in the silt or hide in crevices in the gravel and, although the fish can detect their presence, it takes them some time to extract them all. Thirdly, always use something that is small, dark coloured and has a strong smell that the fish are attracted to. Hempseed and, to a lesser extent, casters are the obvious examples; being inconspicuous, the fish have trouble finding these baits, but the strong attractive smell keeps them looking.

Besides enticing the sought-after fish into the swim, we may also attempt to entice unwanted fish *away* from the swim. Taking advantage of the knowledge that eels are partial to anything meaty, we might employ a very old tactic. This entails tethering a couple of dead fish in some near but out-of-the-way places. Hopefully, the dead fish keep the eels occupied while the angler tries to outwit more worthy adversaries. Small chub may be similarly enticed away and kept preoccupied with a bucket of mashed bread and/or cloud ground-bait.

I have tried experiments to overcome the eel menace by deliberately overfeeding them over the course of three or four days. A measure of limited success has been achieved by this ploy in the wintertime. There probably are, however, far too many hungry eels in the river for this tactic to work in the warmer months – unless you have access to lorry-loads of worms and maggots, and a helicopter to drop them into your swims.

Successful Baits

Hempseed

I buy hempseed in half-hundredweight sacks; the small packs of pre-cooked hempseed, sold in tackle shops, are costly and a waste of time. To achieve a high level of confident preoccupation, especially where big barbel are concerned, takes a lot of feed. As a rule-of-thumb, a gallon of hemp, say, is perhaps sufficient for a summer's day fishing, and half that amount in the wintertime. But I never travel to the river without plenty of back-up stocks; on the day they are really feeding, the last thing you want to do is run out of feed.

Preparing hemp at home is easy, but it does create a lot of condensation, and the aroma is not pleasant. The usual method of preparing hempseed is to simmer it on the stove in a large saucepan or metal bucket. However, it is quicker and better to prepare it in a pressure-cooker, because you get less condensation and smell. Bob James and Ron Chant make theirs, 7lb at a time, in a Baby Burco electric boiler. Whatever the chosen cooking method, pre-soak the hemp overnight in clean cold water, as this will reduce the cooking time considerably. Hemp is ready when the seed starts to split and shows the white inside.

Although, I don't know of a flavour that improves the attractive qualities of hemp, nevertheless I add a few drops of Richworth concentrated sweetener. Ron Chant suggested that if you add a pinch of bicarbonate of soda to the water while cooking, the seed will turn several shades darker, a ploy that might keep the fish looking, and hence in the swim, that little bit longer. And our sweetened, dark-coloured hempseed is a little different from everybody else's.

Unless you know how, it isn't easy to prepare hemp when you are away from home, but Bill Quinlan discovered a straightforward solution to the problem: fill a one-litre Thermos flask three-quarters full with hempseed (Ron and I also make our additions of sweetener and bicarbonate of soda), then top it up with boiling water. Three or four hours later, the hempseed is just right – split and showing the white interior. When on a trip of a few days' duration, the hemp can be cooking in the flask(s) while you are sleeping – a valuable time-saver.

Besides being the premier big-fish attractor, hempseed is a successful hook-bait in its own right, although I suspect that the difficulty of impaling it on a big strong hook deters many anglers. They need not be deterred, however, because there are simple and effective ways to overcome the problem, such as Super-gluing it directly to the hook (see p93).

I suspect that hemp that has been previously prepared and frozen is not so attractive, and thereby as effective, as the freshly prepared variety. Neither am I confident about using ground hemp, except as an ingredient in a paste bait. Used this way, ground hemp is an effective eel repellent. So, nowadays, when making bread-paste, sausage-paste, cheese-paste, or one of the more sophisticated modern pastes, cooked hemp, usually ground to a powder in an old coffee-grinder, is a vital main ingredient.

Paste Baits

Paste baits are made simply by mixing together several ingredients to form an attractive and nourishing fish food. This is not a new idea, of course, but especially now that so many different ingredients are readily available, the possibilities are limitless. Moreover, a successful paste bait can remain exclusive to you and perhaps to a few friends, which may become an important facet on hard fished waters.

Cheese-paste

Bob Buteux has had so much experience and success using cheese-paste that I asked him for his recipe. Here is his interesting reply:

More than forty years have passed since I caught my first chub – a wee fellow of about a pound, from the old River Lea at Cheshunt. The successful bait being cheese-paste.

My fishing pal of that time was Roy Long and our original recipe for cheese-paste consisted of just two ingredients – Cheddar cheese and white bread. This was okay in summer but cold water made it go as hard as a bullet, so we had to experiment. Roy tried Cheddar mixed with plain white flour. On his first outing using the new paste, I popped along to see how Roy was fairing. He was winding in and what had started off as a walnut-sized piece of paste came back hanging on his hook, and looking very much like an onion ring. It took Roy a long time to live down that episode!

Because most of our river fishing was done in the winter, Cheddar was soon discarded. A much better alternative was one of the then new processed cheeses – Kraft Dairy Lea. This wasn't widely available in those days and sometimes we had to visit several shops before striking lucky.

My cheese-paste requires 6oz of processed cheese to each whole loaf. Cut the crust from a tin loaf and discard, the crumb being put in the airing-cupboard to dry out. When dry, mix with water to a stiff paste, then mix in the cheese. (You will find it easier to knock up if both bread and cheese are first separated into four equal parts.) The resulting stickiness can be eradicated by adding fine sausage rusk, which also acts as a binder. The paste is then put in a plastic bag and left for about a fortnight to mature. It must be kept away from dogs, mice, kids etc; my secret hideaway is the top shelf in the garden shed.

After the requisite period you will find it has grown a green mildewy skin, but this can be peeled off, as you would an orange. The paste will now be of a lovely creamy texture, but the smell will be rather overpowering, which can be advantageous – it will deter other anglers from fishing too close to you! On the bank, add either river water or more binder to obtain the desired consistency. You don't, thank goodness, have to make new cheese-paste for every trip, and I've used it as long as seven weeks after making!

Hempseed is added to my cheese-paste when barbel are the specific target. When used for this purpose the hemp is overcooked, so it is all well split and, after cooling of course, is simply mixed in the cheese-paste. Finally, use the water the seed was cooked in to obtain the required consistency.

I will always remember Bill Warren's cheese-paste. It was made primarily from Kraft cheese slices and sliced bread, but was not knocked up to an even consistency. In fact, it was very lumpy, pieces of bread-crust and cheese remaining unmixed. Bill was always reminding me that the size of bait was important; walnut size being about right in most circumstances, he said.

To save all the trouble of making cheese-paste, I once got a friendly local baker to bake me a cheese-flavoured loaf, but this experiment flopped because the resulting flake couldn't be induced to stay on the hook. Nowadays, I'm told, cheese, and other fla-voured loaves are available from supermarkets, etc, and are long overdue an extended trial.

● *Cheese paste accounted for this big chub. Note that the size 4 hook in its lip looks tiny when compared with a chub's mouth*

Sausage-paste

In each of the rivers I have fished, barbel love a paste made from sausage-meat, and pork always seems more productive than beef. To make an effective sausage-paste is simplicity itself. Add either dry breadcrumbs or fine sausage rusk until the stickiness of the meat, when it was bought, is eradicated; about 5oz of breadcrumbs to 1lb of meat is about right. Beware, though, that the paste will continue to harden long after it is knocked up, and cold conditions will harden it even more. Also bear in mind that the more dry ingredients you add, the less the paste's attractive smell will be. This may be countered by adding a few drops of synthetic sausage flavour to the finished paste.

If it is intended to mount the sausage paste on the hook rather than on the hair-rig, you must pick out all the pieces of gristle in the intended hook-bait – a tiresome task but well worth the effort, for a piece of gristle can effectively prevent hook penetration. There is no need to go to this trouble for free offerings or if the paste is to be mounted on the hair-rig. The latter is by far the best way because the use of the hair-rig also allows harder baits to be employed, thereby removing the worry in that respect. Special versions of the hair-rig for paste and seed baits are described on p 93.

Modern specials

Early specials were usually made with a pet-food base such as Kit-e-Kat and, although they were originally intended for carp, these baits turned up some interesting fish of other species. When he was developing bait for carp, Fred Wilton thought a little more deeply about the subject and, working on the theory that all animals need a balanced diet, originated the ideas behind baits that are now termed 'high protein' (HP) or, more correctly, 'high nutritional value' (HNV) baits. This book could be filled with typical recipes and not cover them all, so I will limit my remarks to a few successful ones. Some basic principles apply to the baits which follow and, to avoid unnecessary repetition, will be stated now.

To achieve consistent results, measure all the ingredients very carefully. An ordinary set of kitchen scales will do for the dry ingredients, but for the concentrated flavours you will need a measuring cup or spoon, available from chemists. Take two bowls and mix the dry ingredients in one bowl and the wet ingredients in the other, then mix together the dry and the wet ingredients a little at a time to control the consistency, which needs to be stiffer than might first be supposed. The resulting paste can be used, of course, as bait, and it is as well to remember that paste disseminates its flavour faster than boilies. These days I don't usually bother to make my own boilies; the Richworth Shelf-life range is comprehensive, and I use and recommend these unreservedly. I only make my own when I require a different shaped bait to the universal spherical boily. Mine are cube shaped and made thus: make the paste as above and roll into pancakes ¼in thick, then, with a sharp knife, cut into ¼in cubes before boiling. This ploy has proved very successful but has one disadvantage. Cubes won't catapult as far as balls do, and wind plays havoc when you are trying to bait 'tightly' with a catapult. Neither of these drawbacks matter much in practice on rivers because free offerings are invariably introduced by way of a bait-dropper or swim-feeder.

Always make your bait to the same standard weight; the dry ingredients of my mix equal 16oz (1lb). Working like this makes it easy to determine how much concentrated flavour and/or sweetener to use to maintain consistency. Richworth recommend 5–10ml per pound dry weight for both sweetener and Standard Flavour range, and 3–5ml per pound dry weight for the Blacktop range.

Sodium caseinate paste

Sodium caseinate is a milk derivative, an excellent binder and reasonably priced. These qualities make it almost unbeatable as a basis for any number of paste baits. Again, because of the limitless range of possible ingredients, flavours and additives, there is no need to go any further than to give one example. This particular recipe has proved especially effective for river fish:

> 7oz sodium caseinate
> 6oz ground hemp
> 3oz Casilan
> 5ml Richworth sweetener

Depending on the purpose for which it is required, the desired consistency may be controlled and achieved by the amount of water added. For example, hook-baits don't want to break down too quickly, so hook-bait paste is made quite stiff. On the other hand, it is imperative that ground-bait should attract without overfeeding. Therefore, paste for this purpose must break down quickly, so knock up very dry or soft.

Fish-meal paste

A very easy-to-prepare paste that has been doing 'the business' of late is made from equal amounts of Fish Meal Mix and 50/50 Mix (both from Richworth), and ground-hemp. For ground-bait/pre-bait, just add water, and to stiffen up for hook-bait, also add either wheat gluten or egg albumen.

Boilies

As already stated, I have long given up the tedium of making my own boilies, and use exclusively the Richworth Shelf-life range. My own choice for the majority of my river fishing is the midi-boilie size. To deter eels, though, I use bigger ones on the hook (sometimes two at a time).

Why midi-boilies are not more popular with anglers is a mystery – almost every fish that swims loves them. Furthermore, even a very big fish won't need to eat many large boilies before it becomes satiated, but that same fish will need to eat many more of the midi variety before it reaches the same state. Obviously, the more baits a given fish picks up, the more chance there is of it picking up the one attached to the hook. In other words, the longer our fish spends feeding, the greater the chance you have of catching it.

Richworth midi-boilies are, at last, now available in bulk packs, and two new flavours – White Seed Mix and Pink Seed Mix – have been added to the more established favourites such as Tutti Fruti, Luncheon Meat, Cheese and Strawberry Cream.

For use in conjunction with boilies, there now are available, also from Richworth, feed-inducing rig tablets. These dissolve after casting to rapidly disseminate their flavour. The range includes Aniseed, Cornish Cream, Hemp, Luncheon-meat, Maggot, Raspberry, Strawberry Cream, Tutti Fruti, Vanilla and Wasp-grub. There are some obvious winners on the river among them. Feed-inducing rig tablets may be used in any legering or float-fishing situation. I am also currently experimenting with other new Richworth prod-

ucts, such as bird-food enhancer, worm extract and hemp oil. The latter two have been formulated after a spectroscope analysis of the real thing.

Traditional Baits

I would now like to mention new ideas or novel methods that involve more traditional baits.

Bread

Without doubt, many different kinds of river fish, particularly specimen chub and roach, find bread a compelling bait. Understandably, therefore, it is rare for me to go fishing without a few slices. Perhaps bread's unique construction makes it difficult for the fish to mouth without pricking itself on the hook. But whatever the reasons for its success, bread is too good a bait to ignore, and finding new ways to use it may keep you one step ahead of the rest.

The method of flavouring and/or sweetening a loaf is described on p75, but you can simulate this effect while you are actually on the bank. With an atomiser or spray, the chosen flavour is applied directly to the hook-bait. It is as well to realise that you can get away with stronger flavoured hook-bait than free offerings. Although it may smell attractively, a strongly flavoured free offering may prove unpalatable and hence eventually repel. Probably it will be too late for the fish to reach the same conclusion with the hook-bait! All this applies, of course, to all baits and not just to bread.

A very useful ploy is to use the buoyancy of bread-crust to balance a denser bait. I am convinced that there are many times when a bait fluttering attractively just above the bottom will be taken, when a similar bait fished hard on the bottom will remain ignored.

You don't always have to use a bread-punch when you need to use small fragments of bread on the hook. In fact, on waters where fish may have become wary of punched bread, bread cut into tiny cubes can be more advantageous. Simply steam a slice of white bread over a kettle of boiling water for about 20 seconds, then cut off the crusts prior to flattening the bread with a rolling-pin. With a sharp knife or scissors, cut the bread into small cubes about ⅛in square, and you have a successful alternative to punched bread.

Cheese

The fact that cheese appears to have lost popularity in recent years is puzzling, for it is one of the best chub baits I know. Sometimes a chunk of walnut-size cheese, as Bill Warren advocated, is to the chubs' liking, but generally I prefer to use it much smaller than this. In my experience, ¼in cubes are the right size and you get hundreds of baits from ½lb.

Mounting more than one ¼in cube on the hook together alters the apparent shape of the bait – that is, it disguises the fact that it is made up of cubes. This may just fool a particularly wily chub. Furthermore, the increased surface area of the bait ensures that its flavour is disseminated more rapidly, hence more effectively. This is also a very effective way of using luncheon-meat and does not discount other baits.

Maggots

Maggots can be coloured and/or flavoured to increase their attractiveness to fish. This is not a new idea. The match-fishing fraternity have been doing it for years, but it took some time for specimen anglers to catch on. Perhaps this was because it used to be recommended that colour, etc, was best introduced via the maggots' food and the big-fish man did not want the bother of breeding his own maggots, which would have been his only alternative to control the colour of his own bait. Nowadays, things are so much simpler with the modern flavours and dyes that are so widely available, which can be added to the maggot as bought – an exciting and profitable prospect. Furthermore, there is now no reason to employ older, more dangerous dyes such as the red dye, chrysodine, which was used extensively in the past but which is now known to be probably carcinogenic.

Fishing a large reservoir during the late 1970s, I first became involved in experiments with flavoured maggots. Fished in conjunction with a swim-feeder, the flavoured maggots proved a much more effective bait than identical tactics with unflavoured maggots. Even

when they were fished side-by-side, nine times out of ten the flavoured bait was taken in preference to the unflavoured type.

As soon as the word inevitably spread about the result of these experiments including a very well-known matchman, expressed doubts that the success was in fact due to flavoured maggots. It was argued that as maggots constantly exude ammonia, this powerful solvent would neutralise any attempt at flavouring. This may sound very plausible in theory; in practice, flavoured maggots did the trick then and they continue to account for many big fish caught each season, fish that I am certain would not have been caught on unflavoured maggots.

Rather than buy one colour of maggots, when the going gets harder during the winter, try a mixture. The fish don't seem to mind being fed a combination of red, yellow and white maggots and it gives you variations to try on the hook.

Keeping maggots fresh

During extended summer fishing trips, Thermos flasks are a boon in helping to keep maggots and casters fresh. Ice-cubes, even if they are kept in a large flask, will undoubtedly revert to water after a relatively short period. Nevertheless, the resulting ice-cold water will be useful in keeping the maggot container cool. Another ploy is to scoop out depressions in the soil, in a cool shady place, just big enough for the bait bucket. In such places, the temperature of the soil remains constantly moderate and will do the same for the bait. Ensure, however, that the holes in the bait-box are not masked, because without a good supply of oxygen, maggots will soon suffocate. Also, regularly riddle the maggots changing the medium in which they are kept.

Casters, of course, can be kept fresh for quite long periods, in a previously cooled Thermos flask.

Small bait-boxes are fine for holding small quantities of hook-baits, like worms, sweetcorn, luncheon-meat, etc, and small portions of hook-bait maggots. But don't fall into the trap of filling bait-boxes full to the brim with maggots. Standard maggots, pinkies and squats don't store too well this way. Even if the bait survives, it becomes hot and smelly and will shrink in size. Give live hook-baits plenty of room by selecting a container twice as big as you think you need. Given air, maggots will stay fresh, smell less of ammonia and don't dehydrate.

● *An immaculate barbel for Bill Keal (*Alec Lewis*)*

Sweetcorn

During the early 1970s, when the enormous potential of sweetcorn was widely realised, Bill Quinlan and I were thrilled at the prospect of trying it out on the Royalty barbel. Our hopes were dashed, however, when, despite a season-long and expensive baiting-up programme, we failed to catch a single barbel on sweetcorn, so we gave up and went back to using more productive baits. I was greatly surprised, therefore, when I was on holiday at Christchurch some two or three years later, to witness anglers thumping out barbel from the Great Weir on corn. Obviously, Bill and I had got something wrong! Perhaps we had seriously underestimated how much corn was needed before the barbel accepted it as food. Or perhaps we had not introduced it over a long enough period. Possibly there is some truth in both these theories but, with hindsight, I believe the major mistake was our timing.

Almost every fish with fins loves sweetcorn and smaller, especially less sophisticated fish will greedily consume any quantity of it as soon as it is introduced. Possibly, therefore, such fish may have cleared most, if not all, of the bait Bill and I put in, before the barbel had even begun to feed. Nowadays, in trying to learn from that mistake, pre-baiting is carried out at the time the fish are expected to feed in earnest. In the case of barbel, this will generally be late in the day, not before, say, two hours before dark.

When corn began to lose its effectiveness on the Royalty, my son, Tony, discovered how to extend its life. Tony used a hook-bait of corn together with ¼in cubes of luncheon-meat. These baits were threaded alternately over the hook and up the line for about 2in. Used in this manner, corn continued to produce takes long after most anglers had given up – yet another example that underlines the importance of trying something different.

6
Winter Fishing

Most of my wintertime fishing is spent on the banks of one or other of our rivers in search of barbel and chub, although roach and pike, so long as they are big, can sometimes prove a distraction.

Let me first explain what the term 'winter' on the river means to me: winter has nothing much to do with what date the calendar is showing; wintertime starts for me with the coming of the rains and, within reason, the more rain the better. So long as the river is within its banks, I'm happy. The sight of a river, at the time of a winter spate, continues to stir my blood. The pent-up excitement of eager anticipation knowing what such a scene can mean – a testing battle with lusty barbel and/or chub – often starts me shaking with excitement before the rod has even been put together. Long may it remain so! I realise, of course, that other anglers don't like to fish a river swollen with swirling, coloured water, but I believe that this is because they have not come to terms with the conditions and do not realise what they could be missing.

I am often asked why I prefer to fish the rivers, especially for barbel, in the wintertime, when everybody knows how successful this pursuit can be in the summer. There are many facets to my answer to this query, and I hope that the following will contain enough evidence to persuade you that 'the game is worth the candle'.

As wintertime is less popular with the majority of anglers – and this is especially true at times of spates – there are less people on the riverbanks. This is an important point. It is no use whatsoever to recognise where the fish should be feeding if you cannot try to catch them because somebody is already fishing that swim. Furthermore, to get the best from a winter river, a roving, rather than a static, approach is often necessary. Therefore, fewer anglers means that there will be more swims, hence more options.

Floodwater can, and does, move fish from their usual haunts. At such times the more comfortable water for the fish is much nearer the banks than usual. Often they will be right under the bank in the very margins, obviously near enough for us, the anglers, to show them a bait. And, what is more, when the fish are first in their new surroundings they appear to lose some of their natural caution; perhaps they become disorientated. Whatever the reason, anglers must be ready and willing to exploit the situation.

Fish fight so much harder in wintertime. They appear fitter and the more powerful currents in the river are used by the fish to their advantage. Although more nerve-racking and tiring for the angler at the time, surely this is what river fishing is all about? In the summertime, more often than not you choose the tackle to suit the amount and strength of weed present rather than that which would be sufficient to land the fish. I prefer to fight fish not weed-beds, and in the wintertime, when the weed-beds have died and been washed away, you can choose a more appropriate line strength. Even allowing for the heavier flow that has to be contended with, you rarely need to go heavier than 6lb bs and often you can get away with less.

These days my fishing time is limited, so I cannot afford long periods of inactivity. In wintertime, so long as you do your homework, the results can be so much better for the time spent on the bank. Primarily because there are so many more anglers on the banks, successful summertime river fishing is often a waiting game. You start as early as possible, building up the swim all day, generally hoping to get results in the final hour or so – this all depends on getting the swim in the first place. In wintertime, you move from one likely-looking swim to another, searching out where the feeding fish are, rather than trying to get them to come to you. As

● *Roger Newman with the biggest fully authenticated chub for years; a middle-Avon specimen weighing 7lb 8oz*

● *Dimensions of 29¾ × 19¾in makes this 11lb 14oz barbel, caught by Tony Arbery, one of the best conditioned ever seen by the author*

● *A 5lb 1oz chub is returned by Bob Buteux*

● *Close-up shot of the author's touch-legering technique*

likely as not, so long as you have picked the right place, prepared it properly, and have not frightened the fish in the process of moving into the swim, you will get a bite on the first cast. Surely there cannot be anything more satisfying in angling than to catch fish by using water-craft and by reading the river's surface. And, when successful, as you will be often enough to make the game worthwhile, there cannot be a much better way of building up your confidence.

Finally, if, like me, you keep a record of the weather conditions throughout the winter, not only in your area but also in the areas where the rivers are situated, you are more likely to be able to predict whether a fishing trip will be worthwhile or not. This will not only prove to be a valuable time-saver, but if you, like me, live around 100 miles from your favourite venues, it will save you the considerable cost of travelling. If the weather is doubtful, you can always compromise by fishing a venue closer to home. Then, if the fish are feeding and you consider it worthwhile, travel on to the more distant river.

A rising water temperature, which, more often than not is accompanied by rain, hence coloured water, usually indicates that barbel (and roach) will be more inclined to feed. Conversely, in clearer, and usually colder water, chub (and pike) will more often oblige. Therefore, you can readily see that barbel and chub are a perfect winter combination, because when one is off the feed, more likely than not, the other will be on. There are exceptions, of course – for example, melted snow running into the rivers puts all fish off their food, and it is very difficult if the water is both coloured and cold (by cold I mean about 40°F).

The critical water temperature determining whether your quarry will feed or not will vary and by quite a few degrees Fahrenheit. Obviously, a rising temperature is preferable, particularly when barbel are the target. So long as the water is clear – clear enough, say, to see a half-inch pebble in 4ft of water – you can be confident that chub will feed, no matter how cold the water. As an example, I clearly remember a day spent on the Kennet, near Reading, shortly after the Christmas holidays a few years ago. Snow had laid on the banks for several days, even the margins of the river were frozen and my line was continually being struck by great chunks of ice that were coming down with the current. The reason I remember this particular day so well was that the chub were feeding avidly, and I lost count of how many were caught. The four biggest were all over 4lb!

Water temperature, as one would imagine, is a vital factor in fishing for barbel in winter. For years my friends and I believed that 41°F was the figure that stopped barbel feeding when the temperature was falling and started them again as the water warmed. We have now discovered, however, that this applies only to daylight. After dark is another story altogether. Water temperature as low as 38°F has been recorded on several barbel captures I have witnessed. As a rule-of-thumb, it can be considered that the colder it becomes, the later the barbel will begin to feed and the shorter this feeding session will be. Mild conditions, however, are what I dream of, when the strong south-westerlies blow, accompanied by rain, and the air temperature is in the upper fifties.

Fortunately, events are not always so predictable – for example, let me relate when the Kennet barbel fed in very low temperatures. The weather had been clear and very cold all week. It was so cold, in fact, that the frost had remained all day where the watery winter's sun did not reach it. Because of these conditions chub were the chosen target. Friday's dawn was remarkably beautiful; the river's surface was unruffled by the slightest breeze, and in the smooth sparklingly clear, albeit very cold water, the rose-pink of the early morning winter's sky was faithfully reflected. This gave the illusion that the water itself was pink – a very pretty effect. The pinkness contrasted and yet, at the same time, complemented the crisp whiteness of the frosty banks. I can't put my finger on just what it reminded me of, but the colours in a young girl's complexion would not be too far from the truth. It felt so good to be alive and even better to be out alone on the banks of the Kennet, at the best time of day when most people are still tucked up in bed.

As is my custom, I planned to rove down the river, fishing all the likely chubby holes. Tackle was kept to a minimum. This consisted of a small creel to carry spare essential items of tackle and my provisions for the day: a fold-up seat; a landing-net and a very light quiver-tipped rod. My line was 4lb Specimen Plus tied direct to size 8 spade-end hook.

Many chub obliged during the sunny, but short, mid-winter's day and dusk found me in the most down-

● *Pete Cranstoun has caught no less than seven Kennet barbel over 12lb. This fish, at 12lb 4oz, was his first (*Pete Cranstoun*)*

stream swim on the stretch. This was, and still is, one of my 'banker' big-chub swims, and if I have the stretch to myself for the day, I always leave it until last. Out went a piece of bread-flake which had hardly settled when it was taken with the proverbial bang. This proved to be the best chub of the day, weighing 4lb 12oz. Two more chub quickly followed, then the swim died. The idea of packing up was becoming increasingly attractive, when a steady pull on the line hooked over my finger signalled another bite. After the hook was set, I said to myself, 'If this is a chub, it's a whacker!', but it turned out to be a barbel. It was not of gigantic proportions, but it was big enough to make me want more.

Now, on this stretch of the Kennet (on which, unlike most other parts of the river, night fishing is allowed), most of the proven barbel swims are on the other bank. So, without even waiting to try another cast, I decided to cross over the river to try for the barbel. Long ago I learned to follow my instincts on such occasions and have not often regretted the decision.

In the car, ready for such an opportunity was a bait-box full of diced luncheon-meat. (I never take luncheon-meat cans on to a fishery; a lost or discarded can is unsightly and can cause serious injury to cattle, dogs and other anglers.) After I had collected the meat and stepped up the line to 6lb, I was soon ensconced in a favourite barbel swim. This swim juts out into the river and there is only one way to face, and that is downstream. I can't recall why I struck on the first cast, but as a barbel was hooked it did not bother me too much. On the next cast, my concentration was better and the line gently tightened on my finger, as it does when a small piece of drifting weed fouls the line. I struck more in hope than in anticipation, but another hooked barbel plunged at the end of the line.

Five more barbel were caught by the time I reluctantly packed up around midnight. All gave very small indications, and glycerine (kept for the purpose in an old nail-varnish bottle), continually painted on the rod rings, had prevented the line from freezing to them. Even though my wet landing-net was freezing stiff as a board between captures, the barbel were still feeding. I had to leave then, as arrangements had been made to accompany Tony, my son, on a trip to the Dorset Stour next morning, and I had to get at least a few hours' sleep.

Normally, barbel fishing would have been considered out of the question on such an evening as described. With all the experience in the world at your command, however, you can still be wrong, so it pays to keep an open mind. As Bob Buteux once remarked to me, 'You can't catch 'em if you're at home tucked up in bed!'

Because I find legering to be so much more versatile – that is, almost any swim can be fished effectively – I do not practise float fishing very often in the winter months. And, as the few float-fishing techniques I practise will be described in Chapter 7, there is no need to go into the subject here.

Touch Legering

My favourite method when fishing rivers in the wintertime, touch legering, was first introduced to me by those masters of the art, Bob Buteux and Bill Quinlan, in the 1960s. It is a tribute to its effectiveness with big fish and to the pleasure that I continue to derive from it, that touch legering still holds that position today. Before I discuss how the method works, however, here is a word of warning: to get consistently the best out of fishing, you must not become a slave to any single method. Having said that, I cannot imagine any way to fish that could possibly give me more pleasure than touch legering. Therefore, should the odd catching opportunity be lost, so be it. As long as I am able, in the wintertime you will find me touch legering for chub, barbel and roach, on one or other of our rivers, and long may it remain so.

'You need to use both hands when touch legering' is advice you would do well to ignore. There is absolutely no need to use more than one hand to hold the rod, control the clutch and feel for bites, all at the same time. If this sounds difficult, it isn't. It takes about as much dexterity as tying a shoelace and, once mastered, is never forgotten.

The first essential in touch legering is that you must be seated comfortably. You cannot hold a rod for what may be long periods if you are uncomfortable. The arm holding the rod should be rested on your knee or thigh, whichever you find more comfortable. Use one free finger to hook under the line immediately in front of the reel. It doesn't matter which finger you use, but most exponents of the method use either the index or middle finger.

It is surprising how sensitive are the tips of your

fingers. You don't just feel bites through them; you can tell what the bottom is made up of (there is no mistaking the feel of your bomb on gravel); weed, whether drifting or growing, when it comes into contact with your line transmits different messages; experienced practitioners of touch legering can sometimes even tell the difference in a bite from one species to another; line bites can sometimes be recognised as well. When touch legering, your brain converts the messages received by your fingertips in a similar way to how a blind person reads Braille, only instead of seeing pictures of words in your mind's eye, you get some idea of what is happening beneath the water's surface.

Another fallacy believed by some anglers is that barbel will only give one sort of bite, and that is big. This contention is quite untrue. There are occasions, as will be described later in this chapter, where only big bites from barbel concern us. But these are specialised situations and are far removed from the suggestion that barbel will not, and do not, give small indications of a bite. My own advice, based on twenty-five years' experience, is that barbel (and to a lesser extent chub) sometimes give bites so small that you don't realise that you have had a bite until they let go, and by then, of course, it is too late. And I am willing to bet that any angler legering for barbel has had his bait in his quarry's mouth far more times than he would care to admit, even supposing that he even realised what was going on.

You don't have to take only my word about this. That extremely fine and successful river angler, Tim Norman, writing in the autumn 1990 issue of *Big Fish World*, says, '... barbel will very often take in the hook-bait and reject it without moving. A timely strike in such circumstances, can often result in fish which otherwise might not be hooked.'

I am not making this point so forcibly to prove how clever I am at hitting small bites. The point has to be stressed because of its importance. Once you accept that small bites from barbel are a reality, you can start doing something about them. That something may be intended to make the fish give you a more positive indication – for example, you may try to reduce resistance, or you could go to the other extreme and use a bolt-type rig. This latter option is not so far-fetched as one might imagine; in the opinion of some, in which I include myself, the effectiveness of those very heavy swim-feeders is often due to the fact that they are so heavy and act like a bolt- or shock-rig. In the clearer

● *Ron Chant touch-legering*

conditions of summer, Tim Norman, in the article already referred to, describes how he uses a sight-bob adjacent to the hook to tell when the bait is in the barbel's mouth. There is always more than one way to fool a fish (see Chapter 7)!

When touch legering, a stiffish rod, say 1½lb test, will allow you to feel small bites very well. What you must remember, however, is that using this same rod will allow the fish to feel you equally well. For this reason it pays to use the 'softest' rod you can get away with. Furthermore, when using a quiver-tip in conjunction with a soft rod, the fish hang on just that little bit longer. For years, my favourite touch-legering rod was a little wand with a built-in quiver-tip that Alan Brown made for me. It was originally designed for Kennet roach, but it proved eminently suitable for bigger river fish with a string of big chub and barbel catches to its credit. Then I broke it, so a replacement had to be found.

At about this time, as if in answer to my prayer, I learned of the Drennan range of feeder rods. There are three in the series: Light, Medium and Big. All three come complete with two interchangeable quiver-tips of differing strengths, which are carried, when not in use, in the hollow butt section. These three rods comprise a comprehensive quiver-tipping armoury. My favourite is the Light rod and I use it more than the other two; it is 11ft long and designed to handle reel lines of 2–4lbs bs. As already intimated, however, on occasions I use much stronger lines than this on it and have experienced no trouble. In fact, without wishing to boast, during the 1989–90 winter, a 14lb barbel, besides a string of other hard-fighting river fish, were caught on the Light Feeder equipped with heavier lines than those quoted. What you must remember when using stronger lines than the rod designer intended, is to angle the rod more toward the hooked fish. This throws the strain on the lower, stronger section of the rod. Finally, of course, feeders don't *have* to be used on these rods.

Other Methods

To catch chub and barbel in very high water conditions occasionally demands the use of drastic measures. One such method is known as the beach-caster rig or method. The 12ft of the Big Feeder rod is pointed skywards, supported in a single rod-rest with the butt on the ground. The rod-rest needs to be sturdy (mine is made from an old umbrella pole) and must be set well in the ground, for it will be the subject of considerable stress, as you will see.

The leads to use with this method are the circular ones, shaped like a giant Polo mint, with 'knobbles' on each side, and intended for sea fishing. Sometimes a 1 or 2oz lead will be sufficient to hold the tackle in position, but, if the situation demands it, don't be afraid to use the 4, or even 6oz size. Despite weighing the same, two 2oz leads will hold the bottom better than a single

one of 4oz. My only problem is to find a porter who is strong enough and cheap enough to carry all this weight around for me! Bob Buteux used to do the job, but nowadays he has trouble staying awake long enough to even to walk down to the river!

No matter what size lead you use when fishing dirty floodwater, the tackle won't stay in position for very long. But in practice this doesn't seem to matter much. So long as you can persuade the tackle to withstand the power of the current for, say, five minutes at a time, you are in with a good chance, although ten or fifteen minutes is eminently better, of course. This is not a game for the faint-hearted, however; your rod will be pulled right over, sometimes well past its test curve, but you must sit it out, waiting either for a build-up of rubbish on the line that washes the tackle out of position or until you have a bite.

This is one method where anything but a savage take should be ignored. And, believe me, the takes will be savage – so savage, in fact, that an absolute minimum of a 6lb line is recommended, unless you want to be broken by the power of the bite. There is little in fishing that has such an explosive effect as a barbel bite when fishing the Beach-caster Rig. More often than not, the clutch will be screaming before you have had time to take your hands from your pockets. And, whatever else you may do, don't strike, or you will be sure to crack off. Also, don't sit too far from your rod or take your eyes from it. The sight of your rod taking off like a missile, never to be seen again, is unlikely to make your day, no matter how memorable the event.

Another method where any small indications should be ignored can, for periods, be much more restful, yet no less exciting when the bite comes. I am now talking about possibly the most consistent, and certainly the most popular method on the rivers – the particle-bait/swim-feeder combination. Probably the vast majority of tentative indications, when fishing thus, are line bites. So, unless you want to alarm the fish in the process, anything but deliberate pulls should be dismissed. Proper bites are instantly recognised for what they are, when the tip goes round by about 2ft or more and stays there.

When using the particle-bait/swim-feeder method, I find it preferable to mount the rod(s) in a pair of rod-rests, 'stillwater style'. I sit a little further away than usual, and also sit on my hands to discourage myself from striking prematurely. Sitting back also gives me time to think – I must not strike too hard. It is the easiest thing in the world to break on the strike, when a powerful and heavy fish charges off with the bait, especially when it is fished almost under the rod-top (see also pp 90 and 132).

Winter Baits

If ever circumstances forced me to contemplate fishing for either chub or roach without at least a slice or two of bread in my bag, I don't think I would bother, so highly do I rate bread as bait for these species. Nothing is more versatile and, even allowing for the marvels of modern bait technology, bread-flake is still unique in its consistency. After being in the water for more than a few minutes, flake becomes very wispy, and it is easy to visualise how difficult it must be for a fish to mouth it without pricking itself on the hook.

In the past, a fresh uncut sandwich-tin loaf was used for my flake but, even by looking closely before buying, there was no guarantee that the crumb would be any good for flake or not. Nowadays, I choose the new Hovis, medium-sliced, white loaves, because, provided they are fresh, they prove consistent no matter where in the country they are purchased. These loaves can be flavoured readily, too. As soon as you get one home, carefully open both ends of the wrapping, using two or three squirts of an atomiser spray introduce the chosen flavour at each end. Reclose the wrapping, put the loaf in a polythene bag and place it in the freezer. As the bread thaws out when it is removed from the freezer, so the flavour is drawn throughout the loaf, and much more evenly than one would suspect. Flavours that have proved successful include blue cheese, luncheon-meat, sweetcorn, salmon supreme, and, perhaps surprisingly, tutti-fruity. Flavoured bread has accounted for many big chub for me and is a worthwhile tactic where fish have perhaps become wary of ordinary flake.

Luncheon-meat continues to remain the bait *par excellence* for barbel. This bait is often recommended to be used in big chunks, sometimes the size of a matchbox, but can be even more successful when fished in particle mode. In most situations ¼in cubes are about the right size and it may very well be that more than one such piece mounted on the hook together alters the apparent shape of the bait – that is, it disguises the fact that it is made up of rectangular pieces of meat. This may just fool a particularly wily and wary fish.

As I said in my book *Catching Big Tench*,

Perhaps luncheon-meat should be considered as rather more than a single bait. Surely not all brands are made to the same recipe and, from time to time, it must be prudent for a given manufacturer to change the recipe for one reason or another. Therefore, if you find a brand that works particularly well, buy as much of that batch as you can afford before the recipe is changed or the brand can be no longer obtained.

I speak here from bitter experience learned the hard way.

Hempseed is famed as a barbel attractor and holder, and with good reason. Whenever I choose to use the feeder, at least some hemp is included in the feed. I am not, however, convinced that crushed or ground hemp has anything like the same effect, so I prefer to use the whole seed whenever possible. Maggots and/or caster appear to be the best baits to fish in conjunction with the feeder, of course. But even in the depths of winter, those slimy little horrors, bootlace eels, can drive you to distraction, especially at that bewitching time for barbel – an hour or two either side of nightfall. For this reason I don't use maggots or casters as much as I might, for if the eels continued to pick up my baits at such times I don't think I could trust myself to show them the respect that all fish deserve. KNOW WHAT I MEAN?!!

In coloured water it is almost a waste of time to try to tempt chub with bread-flake, although I don't know the reason for this. What I do know is that you stand a much better chance of catching chub in these conditions if you use cheese or a meaty bait. Luncheon-meat works occasionally but lobworm is *the* chub bait to use in coloured water. I don't understand why it should be so, but often lobworms are more successful if more than one at a time is mounted on the hook; three appears to be the most successful number.

I am also at a loss to explain why sweetcorn appears to lose its effectiveness for barbel in cold water conditions. It is especially puzzling when it is realised that sweetcorn continues to account for many roach and chub each winter.

The one bait that is consistent whatever the conditions is the all-conquering boilie. Chub, barbel, roach,

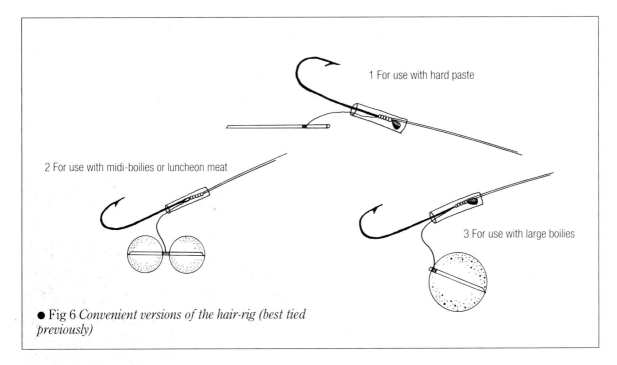

1 For use with hard paste

2 For use with midi-boilies or luncheon meat

3 For use with large boilies

● Fig 6 *Convenient versions of the hair-rig (best tied previously)*

and even the odd pike all love them. Chub, particularly, seem to accept boilies immediately, although a baiting-up programme is better, of course. Invariably I fish midi-boilies in large, open-ended feeders, with both ends of the feeder plugged with ground-bait. Because the boilies need to be released from the feeder quickly, the ground-bait is mixed as dry as possible and the feeder is given a good jerk as soon as it has settled.

What I cannot determine is whether the use of the hair-rig increases one's chances when river fishing. So far, I am not convinced that the hair-rig has anything like the effect in running water that it has in stillwater, but see Fig 6 for suggested and convenient hair-rigs.

Floodwater Success

From time to time respected anglers recount their experiences of a feeling or premonition of when and/or where to fish. Richard Walker has written about the sixth-sense he developed while carp fishing. This, when experienced by Dick, proved utterly reliable. Then Roger Baker, writing in *Barbus* (the Barbel Catchers Club magazine) tells of how, when fishing for (and catching) some big tench, the feeling came to him that

he ought not to be tench fishing, but that he should be out on the River Ouse in search of big barbel. Roger obeyed his instincts, and that very evening he caught his biggest barbel to date – 12lb 2oz.

I, too, have felt that irresistible urge to fish, come what may. Although 'my' sixth sense is not 100 per cent reliable, the following is perfectly true, and my instincts on this occasion did not let me down. These events occurred a long time ago – on the evening of 13 December 1979 – but the memory of them is as fresh as ever.

The rains had come at last and with a vengeance, Wales and the Westcountry were flooding over a wide area. My friend, who (to prevent him further embarrassment) shall remain anonymous, could not face the weather and phoned to cancel. On most occasions when conditions were so inclement, this would have been enough excuse for me to cry off too, but not this particular evening, for the feeling I had was especially strong.

My old van lumbered westward on the M4 in a cloud of spray, and not for the first time I questioned my sanity. Just after I left the motorway, the road was flooded in a dip. I did not notice this until it was too late and the engine died as a cascade of water drowned the electrics. I spent an unpleasant half-hour mopping up, during which time the rain poured down my neck and spray from a hundred other vehicles washed all over me. Eventually, the rain god smiled in my direction, and with a prayer from me, my van staggered on into the sodden blackness.

My swim was situated at least three-quarters of a mile from the nearest access point and, even though I wore a Barbour jacket over a waterproof suit, together with waders, the torrential rain found every chink in my protection.

Eventually, just as I was settling down with my two rods lying in their rests, the betalights gleaming eerily and my seat positioned comfortably under my umbrella, my stool collapsed. There was no alternative – I had to return all the way to the van to fetch the spare.

Although I was wet when I first arrived at the river,

● *The author's first Dorset Stour double-figure barbel at 11lb 2oz*

I was soaked through after I had walked back the second time. However, bloody-minded determination was driving me on now and I was intent on fishing that night, whatever else fate had in store for me.

One rod was swing-tip armed, the other was quiver-tipped; the former was lowered in the very margin, the latter held a quarter of the way across, aided by a ½oz bomb. The bait on both was luncheon-meat. Within a very short time the swing-tip indicated a positive bite and a heavy barbel was hooked. Unfortunately, after a short struggle it fell off. I was engaged in rebaiting this rod, when the quiver-tip on the other rod was pulled over a good foot. A desperate lunge was made for it, but I missed. Having put the quiver-tip rod to one side, luncheon-meat on a size 6 spade-end hook, tied direct to a 6lb line, was replaced exactly where the first hooked fish had been lost. Ten minutes later the swing-tip fairly flew up, and again I was into a barbel. This time no mistake was made and the torch-light revealed a beautiful fish of 8lb 6oz, length 27½in.

Once again I rebaited with the pink and it was accurately positioned in the successful spot. Half-an-hour passed uneventfully, except that the Kennet was now showing signs of all the rains it had absorbed.

Two further mishaps occurred to test my resolve. The first was that my bright 420 micro-lambert beta-light on the quiver-tip rod, lying at my side, decided of its own volition to leap into the murky depths of the river, never to be seen again. The other misfortune was that in the intense darkness I had not noticed that a very large puddle had formed in the lap of my Barbour. The initial emotion I felt was one of shock as the zips on both Barbour and suit were suddenly breached by icy water. Instinctively I leapt to my feet, which was a mistake, for as I did so the cold water cascaded in freezing rivulets down both my legs to fill my waders to a depth I previously would not have thought possible.

My system was just recovering, when the swing-tip gave a small, yet positive lift. However, it fell again almost immediately. 'Do that again and I'll have you,' I said aloud to myself. My hand hovered over the butt. The tip lifted and held; I had hooked him.

This fish did not fight half as well as the first and was soon in the landing-net. And yet, as I lifted the barbel out I knew that at long last a twelve-year quest was over. By the light of the torch my balance confirmed my suspicion. After allowing for the weighing-bag, I entered the weight, 10lb 3oz,'against her in my diary. It was my first double-figure barbel.

I tried to fish on, but by now the river was carrying so much rubbish that I found it impossible. Having telephoned my wife, we felt that it would be unfair to bring our young son out to photograph my prize – not under those conditions and not at that time of night – so it was photographed on the retaining sack. At 31½in long it made a splendid sight, and for my own satisfaction I need no photograph of it, for its picture will burn brightly in my mind's eye for ever.

At the pull of the button my van started first time for the homeward journey. Sometimes, at the end of the day, despite all the trials and tribulations, it all seems worthwhile.

Postscript

Less than two months later I was fortunate enough to take a second double from the Kennet. Conditions on this occasion were very different from those described above and, as it was the weekend, my son Tony accompanied me (Tony caught a 7-pounder). So, after more than twelve years' trying, I finally got two doubles in less than eight weeks. The fish proved to be different individuals and although the weights were similar (the first weighed 10lb 3oz, the second 10lb 2oz), the latter fish was 1in shorter at 30½in long.

Twitch Bites

More than twenty years have slipped from time's reel since twitch bites first came to my attention. It all started at the Royalty Fishery, on the Hampshire Avon.

The weather was typical of the days my friends and I choose to fish for barbel in winter: there was a stiff south-westerly wind accompanied by showers and an air temperature in the fifties. However, on this particular day the barbel were proving unco-operative. Bites were few and far between.

Up until this time I believed that a barbel bite while touch legering was a deliberate affair. When feeling the line for them, a positive pull alerted you to the savage, rod-wrenching old-fashioned barbel bite that was 100 per cent sure to follow. (How I wish the same could be said today.)

On the day in question, Bill Quinlan and I were on

holiday midweek because the weather looked so promising for the Royalty barbel. Our style was (and still is) largely a roving affair, whereby we try a cast or two into any likely spot. We had the fishery to ourselves, so we took one bank each. That way we wouldn't waste time fishing a swim that one or other of us had already tried. By midday, I still hadn't had a bite, so I decided to have a chat with Bill.

After crossing from the west bank, by way of the pipe-bridge, I made my way downstream to the Railway Pool in which Bill was fishing. He invited me to join him in trying to hit some strange bites he was getting. 'Don't know what they are,' he said, 'They're heavy donks, but quick. There and gone.'

As I positioned my stool silently next to Bill's, he struck, and the look of astonishment on his face was a picture as he realised that he had hooked a barbel of 8lb plus.

For the remainder of that day we sat it out in the Railway Pool. Between us we struck more than a hundred times, sometimes only at what we thought were bites. Some of the small indications were indeed bites, and to prove that the first fish was no fluke, we caught five more barbel. Using bread-crust as bait, each one was caught by striking at the sharp bite described.

From that day onward, twitches, as these bites came to be called, became more and more usual. Indeed, there is nowadays (and has been for years) a stretch of the Kennet where I find that the good old-fashioned barbel bite is a thing of the past. Perhaps the reason is that this particular water contains the most educated barbel I know of. Both matchmen and pleasure anglers, in addition to big-fish men, have for years recognised the potential of this venue. Consequently, the fish there, not only barbel, have become very wary.

Not all small bites are from suspicious fish, however; some of the tiniest bites are given by fish feeding confidently. It isn't always easy to tell one from the other, but there are occasions when you can differentiate. (To come to terms with these tiny bites with any degree of consistency, necessitates touch legering. We have already seen that there are occasions when it is vital to use a different approach, but when you want to know what is happening below the surface, with any degree of certainty, but you can't actually see anything, it is essential to hold the rod and feel the line.)

The confident twitcher often gives a bite which is not unlike weed hitting the line. There are, however, two distinct differences: when the bait is lying near streamer weed, the line is being struck constantly by the fronds. This is unlike when a barbel is responsible, for a fish only gives intermittent indications and usually not more than one per cast. The other difference is that on carefully retrieving the tackle, after such an indication, the bait is rarely recovered intact, which can only mean that the bait has been right down the barbel's throat, to its very teeth. Nowadays, when this happens I change to a hair-rig or a bristle-rig, which sometimes sorts them out.

Often, the wary twitcher gives a single, hard tug. And, as so often it is unexpected, it can be one of the most frustrating bites to come to terms with. Trying the upstream leger, in swims where this method is possible, can often solve the problem. Perhaps reducing resistance is the key to the problem, but – and I have proved this to my own satisfaction – in swims where it is impossible to upstream leger, wary twitchers can be caught on exactly the opposite tack – a bolt-rig. For this fishing, I use at least a 1½oz bomb, and the hook-link is no longer than 2in and, occasionally, even as short as 1in.

I have heard it said, and I have also read, that some anglers only write about twitchers to enhance their reputations. The argument given is that because these writers have, to a greater or lesser extent, come to terms with these bites, they are the better anglers. This is absolute nonsense.

For my own part, I talk and write about twitchers, for therein lies the problem. Big bites are beautiful and no angler, no matter who, needs to be told how to recognise one or what his reaction to one needs to be. There is no self-interest in this at all. Small bites are the problem, so if I can help (or get help) to sort them out by writing about them, then this is my motive.

Twitch bites are not confined to the winter, of course. I well remember Bob Buteux and I fishing for summer barbel in the middle reaches of the Hampshire Avon. Fishing with a block-end feeder and maggots, we often noticed barbel in the swim. Sometimes the fish approached right up to the feeder and/or hook-baits, and in the majority of cases gave no discernible indication of a bite. At the time I felt that the barbel were picking up our baits, but so tentatively that we could not tell. Although the waters of the Avon at that time of the year are pretty clear, even with the aid of bright sunlight, and though we were wearing polarising sunglasses, our hook-baits could not be seen. So, whether we were getting bites or not remained a theory.

On another visit to the same stretch, Bob and I bumped into an old friend, Lee Kitchen. During that day, Lee's pal, Dave, fished for some large barbel that he could see, using a swim-feeder and canned sweetcorn as bait. He was not doing very well when Lee came along to see how his friend was getting on. On entering Dave's swim, Lee observed the barbel behaving similarly to the ones Bob and I had seen previously. However, Lee and Dave held one advantage over Bob and myself: they could clearly see the brightly coloured sweetcorn hook-bait.

Dave fished on, while Lee observed and commentated on what was going on below the surface: 'A biggie has emerged from the far weed-bed.... It's mopping up the loose corn.... now it's approaching the feeder... it's right on the bait.' 'Strike!' yelled Lee. But Dave remained unmoved, for he had not seen, or felt, any indication of a bite. Lee saw the barbel move away from the bait and return to the sanctuary of the weed-bed. After ten minutes or so of no further action, Lee suggested a new cast. This Dave did.

'Right, here it comes again... now there's two of them ... no, he's turned downstream.' Lee's commentary continued. 'The other one's showing interest now ... he's approaching the bait slowly; as if cautious... he's near now.... within about a foot... six inches.... he's on the bait.' 'Strike!'

This time Dave did as he was ordered and his rod assumed its battle curve. The result was an 8lb 14oz middle Avon barbel, hooked fair and square in the mouth.

Three more barbel were forthcoming to Dave's rod, hooked under similar circumstances to the first one. Dave swears to the fact that none of them gave the slightest indication at his end. For the record, those fish all weighed over 7lb apiece. On this same day I caught two barbel from the opposite bank. Both gave big bites.

I could quote many more similar incidents, but just one more will suffice. This occurred near Newbury on the Kennet. A piece of luncheon-meat was cast into a hole in the weed. Within a few minutes I experienced the ultimate bite thrill in angling – an old-fashioned barbel bite – and my catch weighed 6lb 14oz. On the next two or three casts a tentative twitcher plucked at the bait, but the barbel did not hang on long enough for the strikes to connect.

The rod, because of the heavy weed growth, was a light carp rod. This, I thought, might be providing too much resistance by being too stiff in the tip, so I changed to one armed with a quiver-tip. On the next cast the barbel which weighed 6lb 6oz held on a little longer. Two barbel of similar size, from the same swim on the same day and on the same bait, gave vastly differing bites. So there seems to be no hard-and-fast rule.

That some barbel anglers still get a majority of big bites to small, I don't dispute, but I can only describe with any authority the experiences of my immediate circle of friends and my own. Trefor West has promised me a trip with him to fish for some barbel that don't know what a twitch bite is, and I am looking forward to that opportunity.

Finally, do not be misled into believing that only barbel are capable of giving twitch bites – nothing could be further from the truth. Fish of all species are capable of them. And do not think that all small bites are twitch bites. Remember that many small fish, as well as crayfish, etc, will generally only give small indications. Differentiating between various kinds of small bites will only come with experience, and there are no short-cuts. You have to find out for yourself and, that, surely, is part of the fun. I know that I would not have missed this particular learning curve for anything.

● *Bill Quinlan's biggest 'twitcher' to date – 12lb 1½oz*

7
Summer Fishing

Whenever conditions are right – that is, low and clear water coupled with bright sun and little or no wind – and these coincide with any free time I might have, I will be out on the riverbank endeavouring to find fish of a size that interest me. This is a very important activity in my calendar, for once their whereabouts are known, I can fish much more confidently. Of course, there is no more certain way of knowing that the stamp of fish you seek exist than by seeing them with your own eyes.

Taking advantage of this means that my practice of river fishing in summertime is completely different from the winter style described in the previous chapter. What is the point of the 'roving' approach if the whereabouts of the fish is already known? You should know from your observations where the fish live and feed, so the longer and more often you can fish the correct place, the more likely you are to succeed.

One of the most common mistakes made by the inexperienced angler is to dismiss a swim too early. It seems that they often get the choice of swim right in the first place, sit it out all day, then, toward dusk, when the chances of success are highest, they leave, having lost heart or their confidence. Mistakenly, they believe that the swim is a 'non-producer' and, more likely than not, rarely go back to try there again.

Plainly, this is a gross mistake, for a single fishless day, in the great scheme of things, is much too short a time on which to base any conclusions. A far better approach in summer, once the fish are found, is to fish that swim, or area, at every available opportunity. You should not give up before the situation absolutely dictates that you must, either because the rules prohibit fishing on into darkness or you really have to go home. One of my friends taught me the benefit of fishing on to the very last second of the day. It was only when everything else had been packed away, including his rod-rests and landing-net, that then, and only then, would he take his bait(s) from the water. You would be surprised how many bonus big fish have been caught just by employing this extremely simple tactic.

However, although I am recommending that one swim should be fished as often as possible, you must still keep an open mind and be prepared to try anything that might promote success. In other words, although doggedness and persistence are great attributes for a big-fish angler to possess, complacency and dogmatism should be avoided.

Another mistake the unwary angler can easily make is to fish a swim prematurely. It is understandable that once a big fish is spotted, the angler wants to get his bait to it as soon as possible, but such action is likely to spook all the big fish in the area and so deter them from feeding. As pointed out in Chapter 3, a bait-and-wait approach is more appropriate and much more likely to end in success. Don't forget, when the fish can actually be closely observed, it is much more straightforward to determine exactly where the bait should be positioned with the best chance of being picked up and exactly when to begin fishing proper.

The time to begin fishing is when the biggest fish present are feeding avidly. Impatience to cast before this stage is achieved most likely will only ensure that the biggies will not be caught that day. Inexperienced anglers will then make the mistake of believing that the fish were not hungry and put their lack of success down to that reason.

Of course, there are days when observed fish cannot be tempted whatever is tried, but it is my belief, based on years of close and careful observation, that this lack of response is most likely due to a mistake by the angler. It may be that the wrong bait has been used or that the choice of tackle was wrong. The fish might have been aware of your presence because of a clumsy movement or an inappropriate choice of clothing that allowed the fish to see you. But it might not even have been your fault – for example, the fish could have been scared previously by someone or something else. In fact, there are a number of different reasons why fish don't bite, but rarely is it that they are not hungry. So every detail must be considered very carefully. For example, it is no use choosing the best of drab clothing and make every move as slowly and silently as possible, only to scare every fish within a mile by banging in an umbrella pole with a rock.

After years of observing barbel in their natural habitat, I have been forced to conclude that the biggest members of a shoal are also the most dominant. But this does not necessarily mean that the biggest fish will be at the front of the shoal. What it does often indicate is that the biggest fish has first choice of the richest part of the feeding ground. Very likely this is the part of the swim closest to the bank. The moral is clear when

legering: unless there is absolutely no option, do *not* cast your feeder and hook-bait; it is much better to lower it accurately in position. Besides all other considerations, this means that you can still feed accurately, and place your hook-bait spot-on, even after the sun has set. No matter how good at casting you are, there is no better way than this to ensure that your feed and hook-bait(s) are in exactly the right place every time.

● *Hooked while long-trotting during a match, this Hampshire Avon specimen led Dave Swallow a merry dance before breaking free*

Float Fishing

I usually only resort to float fishing rivers in areas that I cannot leger effectively. Classic examples include sunken trees, when a carefully controlled and guided float will allow you to search right in among the submerged branches. Overhanging trees and bushes, with not enough flow beneath them to carry in the lightest leger, may also be tackled effectively with a float. Long-trotting a float may also allow a bait to be presented to areas that are inaccessible or too far away to be reached by any other method. And, being the most sensitive method yet devised, the float can also be tried when delicate bites are at their most frustrating.

Reels and lines

My float fishing set-up is kept as simple as possible and the same basic set of tackle is varied to suit differing conditions. In my tackle-room are several good quality centre-pin reels, but they are rarely used. I find that my Shimano 2500 Bait-runner fixed-spool reels suffice for the little float fishing I practise. With the bail-arm open, line flow may be controlled with the fingers of the hand holding the rod. The middle finger of the same hand traps the line on the spool when striking.

Of course, line strengths are picked to suit varying conditions and/or different species. To enable a quick change from one strain to another, you need to carry a number of different interchangeable reel spools, each loaded with a particular line. If a particular reel design offers both shallow and deep spools, so much the better. Three or four of each will provide enough scope to cover most types of river fishing. The average big-fish angler might own seven or eight spools for each reel. Here is a typical selection to get the optimum usage.

1 Deep spool, 20lb line for pike fishing close to snags.
2 Deep spool, 14lb line for general pike fishing.
3 Deep spool, 10lb line for legering for barbel, carp, etc, in dense weed or close to snags.
4 Deep spool, 8lb line for heavy feeder fishing, up to 3 or 4oz.
5 Deep spool, 6lb line general feeder and other leger work.
6 Shallow spool, 4lb line legering and float fishing for chub and/or roach.

7 Shallow spool, 2½lb for heavy waggler floats.
8 Shallow spool, 2lb floating line for light waggler and stick-float fishing.

In addition, it is also a good idea to double up on the spools loaded with the most used lines. In my case, in summer, this would mean at least two spools loaded with 10lb, 6lb and 4lb breaking strains. The last thing you want to be doing when the fish are 'mad on', is to be winding new line on your reel, even supposing that you had any with you. Of course, there is no need to carry all your spare spools on to the riverbank with you all the time. It is only necessary to take the ones you are likely to use; the others may be left in your car for use in an emergency or in an unprecedented and/or unpredicted situation.

Floats

In turbulent rivers like the Hampshire Avon, it is essential to use floats that will support at least seven AA shot or thereabouts. And too many anglers fishing this river make the mistake of trying to use too light a float. For example, the patterns I choose from, for much of this work, are either a No 4 Crystal Avon or, for more stability, a stick-float, with either a lignum, nylon or wire stem, depending on the job in hand.

Lignum stems are more weighty and open up a greater casting range to the stick-float. This material is surprisingly versatile and as long as the balance between the body material and stem is correct, floats loaded with this wood can be used for on-the-drop, trotting and holding back. This is the float to use when fishing beyond two or three rod lengths and it can be controlled effectively for up to twice this distance. You get the same presentation obtained with a cane stemmed stick but at further range.

Nylon stems are slightly heavier than cane or fibreglass and give better presentation when trotting at the speed of the current in slightly faster water. The heavier stem prevents the float rising up or lying flat when the bait needs to be slowed against the flow. This is a good pattern for fishing over-depth and edging the bait through inch by inch, often a tactic which brings extra fish toward the end of a session.

Wire-stem sticks are the best pattern to use in boily water. They are very stable and can be used to beat awkward drift and a downstream wind. The wire is the stabiliser that gives greater control. They cock quite

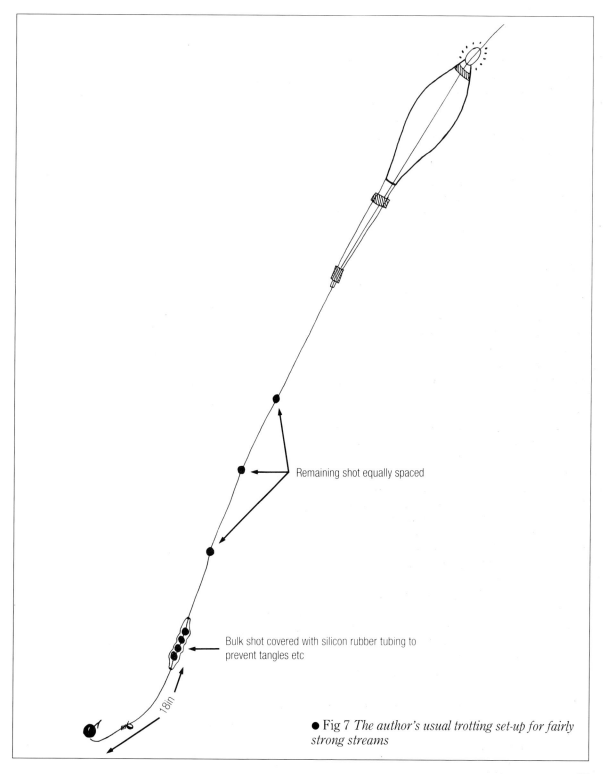

Remaining shot equally spaced

Bulk shot covered with silicon rubber tubing to
prevent tangles etc

18in

● Fig 7 *The author's usual trotting set-up for fairly
strong streams*

quickly, which can be a bonus when you are on a lot of fish and fishing a heavy bulk shotting, as described below. This set-up can also prove successful when you need to be selective, because you can put your hook-bait through nuisance fish to reach better specimens. Again, this pattern is less prone to riding up when it is held back hard.

Shotting patterns in this type of water are also important, and my usual set-up has three AA shot bunched 18in above the hook; the remaining AA shot is equally spaced out above this bulk. The reason for this shotting pattern is that it provides sufficient loading low down so that no matter how hard the float is held back, the bait will not rise too far off the bottom. Big roach and barbel especially, appear to prefer the bait quite close to the bed of the river.

Tangles can be caused when the line wraps itself around between the bulk shotting. It can also lead to line twist. To prevent this, slip a snug-fitting length of silicon-rubber tubing over the bulk shot. This set-up has other advantages, too: it helps to keep the shot in place, preventing any loss in weed-beds or retrieving tackle from snags; and, when using hempseed, it prevents fish taking the shot in mistake for the bait, so lessening the occurrence of false bites.

Legering

For me, summertime legering invariably means using a pair of rods, set in rests, together with swim-feeder tactics – in fact, a fairly standard and straightforward set-up. However, this does not mean that you can stop thinking and/or experimenting. Take for example that simple, yet most effective piece of equipment, the swim-feeder. In that excellent publication, *Improve Your Coarse Fishing*, Kevin Wilmot expressed my own thoughts so succinctly that I have reproduced them here:

Although there are literally dozens of different types on the shelves of most good tackle shops, there are probably *hundreds* of different ways in which they can be adapted to suit various fishing conditions.

Modern feeders are very good, and will allow you to catch fish in most feeder-fishing situations, but the best anglers are those who are prepared to adapt

their tackle to score when the going gets tough. Here are a few simple ways in which shop-bought feeders can be 'changed' – and they take only a few seconds to do.

Different Weight
All shop-bought feeders come with some sort of weight attached to them, clipped to the side, inside, or hanging from the bottom. Both size and position of this weight can be altered in seconds. Small, clip-on weights are available whose ends push into holes in the feeder body. By adding or subtracting clip-ons exactly the right weight can be achieved.

Altering the position of the weight on the feeder can also affect its performance. A feeder with a weight in the form of a metal strip of heavy material along one side will hold bottom in flowing water much better than one whose weight hangs from the bottom or is inside. These two latter types of feeder will cast better, however.

Different Size
Using small scissors to carefully cut the size of a feeder will reduce the amount of bait it holds. On cold winter days, for example, some block-end feeders will have the capacity for too many maggots. Cutting the feeder back so it holds 10 or so maggots will ensure a regular if meagre supply of bait to your swim. Even large feeders can be cut right back if a heavy weight is still required.

They can be cut back to just about any size – even just the two end caps with a very short piece of plastic between them, making the feeder into little more than a link-leger with an added feed compartment.*

Bigger Holes
Enlarge the holes in a feeder using a special hole enlarger available from most tackle shops. This allows your bait to escape faster which can be an advantage if bites are coming fast or if the water is so cold that the bait wouldn't escape if the holes were left their normal size.

Another way of enlarging holes is to cut out the plastic between two of them, making an oval shape.

---

* Another situation for using a cut-down feeder is when a large fish is feeding alone. You may very well soon overfeed it if you don't cut down the amount of feed.

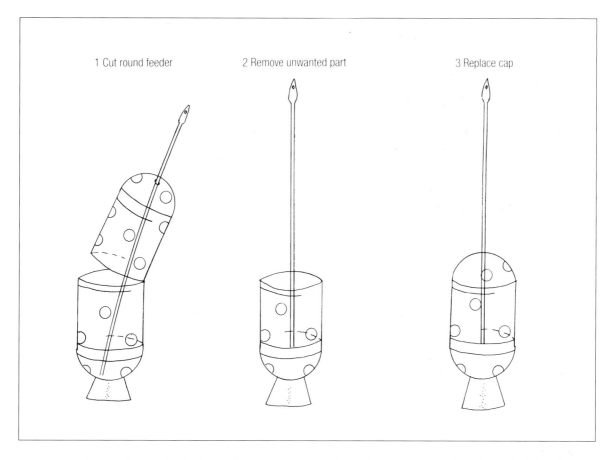

1 Cut round feeder   2 Remove unwanted part   3 Replace cap

Discard the small length of plastic between the holes. This is best done on the diagonal which helps the feeder maintain its strength, and toward the top end of the feeder rather than the bottom end. This will mean less spillage of bait from the feeder during preparation for casting, and as the top end of the feeder normally becomes the downstream end, the bait will escape that much faster.

Different Link

Altering the length of the link from your feeder can make a dramatic difference to your catch rate. A feeder attached to a long link will undoubtedly attract more bites than one attached to a short link, but more bites will be successfully hit with a short link.

The answer is to experiment until just the right combination is achieved.

Think of all the alterations you often have to make to your float tackle to keep in touch with fish during

● Fig 8 *Simple feeder modification to hold less bait*

a session. Treat feeder fishing the same by making changes to the size, type and weight of your feeder, the way it is attached to your line and the length of the link. Your results can only improve.

Rigs for use with block-end feeders

Rigs for use with block-end feeders are many and varied, and range from simple to more complicated set-ups. Reliability is the key, wherever you are fishing. When you are on a big river fishing a big feeder, for example, use a leger stop, as described on p 54 to stop the feeder dropping all the way to the hook. In weedy waters, such as the Dorset Stour and the Hampshire Avon in summer, it would be better to avoid swivels altogether. They can easily become clogged up and ruin the effectiveness of the rig. Much more suitable is a

● *The biggest Kennet barbel of recent years – Pete Cranstoun's 13-pounder*

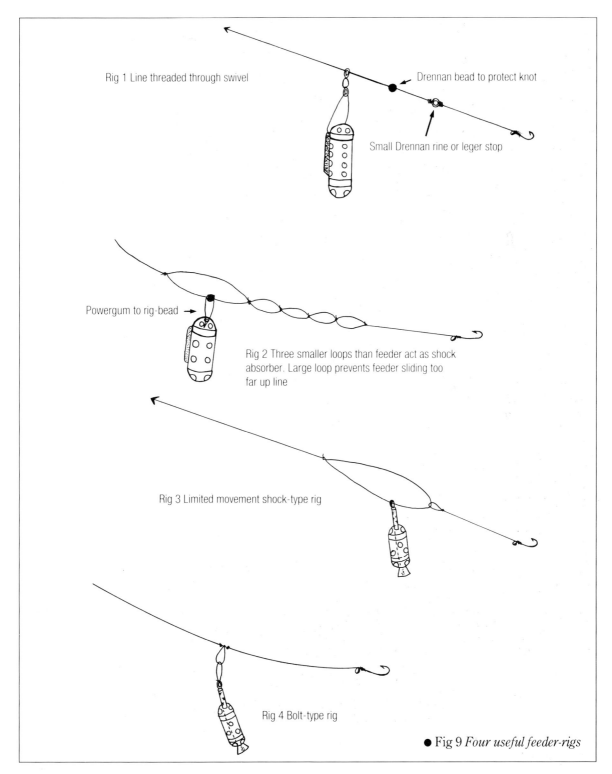

Rig 1 Line threaded through swivel

Drennan bead to protect knot

Small Drennan rine or leger stop

Powergum to rig-bead →

Rig 2 Three smaller loops than feeder act as shock absorber. Large loop prevents feeder sliding too far up line

Rig 3 Limited movement shock-type rig

Rig 4 Bolt-type rig

● Fig 9 *Four useful feeder-rigs*

small Drennan ring. Illustrated in Fig 9 are diagrams of four useful block-end rigs.

Beating floating weed

As a result of the almost continuous weed-cutting on the Hampshire Avon, in summertime that river is notorious for floating debris and weed coming down with the current. When legering, with or without a feeder, this rubbish can create massive problems, causing false bites and a build-up on the line until your terminal tackle is dragged out of position.

One way around this is to sink the line and top section of the rod completely beneath the surface, and point your rod straight at the bait on the bottom and touch leger. You will soon become proficient at differentiating between false and proper bites.

If the floating weed problem is not too serious, you can still fish a pair of rods in their rests. Just position the

rests so that the rod-tops are submerged as described above.

Bite detection

Bite detection when legering the rivers in the warmer months is often straightforward – the quiver-tip is usually pulled right round, and nobody needs to be told what their reaction to this should be. When, however, small bites are a problem, such as when uneducated barbel, say, are the target, it is best if you can see the bait. The benefits of this are twofold: small or unwanted fish can be avoided, and you can see when the fish you seek has the bait in its mouth. A timely strike then can hook a fish before it has time to eject the bait.

When dark-coloured baits, such as hemp and casters, are used they can rarely be seen on the bottom of the swim. This is when a clever tactic, introduced to me by those two fine and very successful anglers, Terry

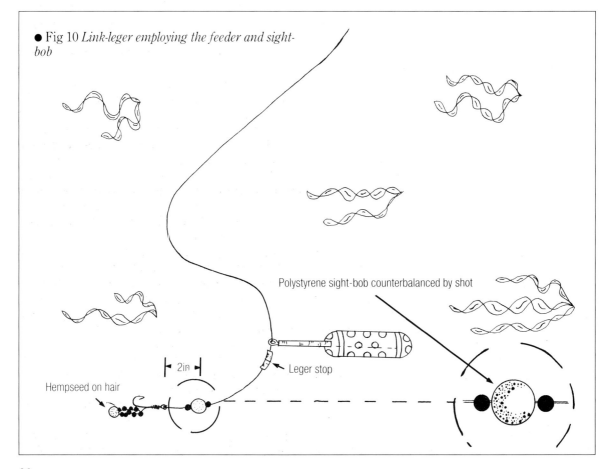

● Fig 10 *Link-leger employing the feeder and sight-bob*

Polystyrene sight-bob counterbalanced by shot

Leger stop

2in

Hempseed on hair

Lampard and Tim Norman, comes into its own. Two inches from the hook a small white piece of polystyrene is fixed to the line by a shot either side so that it just sinks. The size of the polystyrene is dictated by its visibility on the bottom. Although the bait cannot be seen, its precise position is known. As soon as the sought-after fish's mouth is over that spot, watch the marker; if it moves, strike, for this indicates that the bait has been picked up.

The Fox Swinger

A recently introduced bite indicator that I have been experimenting with and have great hopes for is the Fox Swinger. This is a revolutionary new bite and drop-back indicator that is suitable for all leger fishing applications, in either still- or running water. The adjustable weight can be set anywhere between zero and 28g to allow for any type of legering, including free-lining, upstream legering and long-range fishing. It will instantly and positively show a take without the resistance associated with other outdated, bobbin-type indicators.

The Swinger is easily attached to any rod-rest or buzzer simply by fixing the permanent top unit. This enables the angler to attach readily or remove the Swinger quickly. The Swinger can be transported on the rod-rest while moving swims, etc.

Because of its sensitivity and lack of resistance, the Swinger differentiates between takes and line bites, as a line bite will cause it to rise gently and then fall back to its original position without frightening a line-shy fish.

In use, after casting, position the Swinger head on the line and allow it to fall with a sliding weight set at its lowest position. When all the slack is taken up, reposition the weight to balance out the pull of the current for ultimate sensitivity.

The Fox company supply a variety of equipment, such as different heads, additional weights, etc, all of which help to make the Swinger one of the most versatile bite indicators that I have used. Of course, Swingers can be used in conjunction with buzzers, for audible as well as visual indication, and the heads have provisions for a betalight for after-dark fishing.

Pre-baiting

As already explained in Chapter 3, swim preparation is vital toward achieving consistent success, and pre-baiting is the most important aspect of this success. Wildlife – and fish are no exception – comes to food in increasing numbers, (feed the birds in your garden for a week and see), but pre-baiting must be carefully considered if you are to get the best from it.

Observation is the key to just where in the river to introduce the feed. Relatively, there are just a few places in a given stretch where big fish regularly feed, and you have no choice but to locate these places first, otherwise the chances of catching big fish consistently will be remote. Let us consider a typical example after locating some feeding barbel.

Observe their movements closely and don't be too impatient to fish for them. Barbel usually approach their feeding area from downstream, working their way slowly up the swim to the top end. Then they will turn, drifting down well below the swim before repeating the process. Very often there will be one, usually small, spot in the swim where feeding is more intense, and an individual fish will return unerringly again and again to that spot. The best time to introduce the free offerings is when the barbel are almost at the end of their drift downstream.

Not all individuals feed on the same preferred spot; in fact, it would appear that some of the biggest individuals within a shoal each have their own favourite feeding spot and rarely encroach on another's feeding patch. At the downstream end of the patrol, these larger fish appear to arrange themselves at an appropriate distance out from the bank and return upstream on 'lines' that coincide with their preferred feeding spots in the swim. No angler will mistake the significance of this fact when first the free offerings and, later, the hookbait itself are positioned. And these must be positioned very accurately – a few inches one way or another can be the difference between abject failure and spectacular success – so the bait must be placed rather than cast. A word of warning, though – don't try to move the hookbait when the fish are near as you will spook them. It is far better to wait for their drift downstream before any repositioning is attempted.

The importance of very careful observation cannot be overstressed; individual fish feed differently, and feeding patterns will change from day to day and from swim to swim. Note how long they remain in the swim; where *exactly* are the suspected hot-spots, which the biggest fish prefer; are the barbel aware of your bait and are they feeding on it, or are they just grubbing about in general, as they were before the free offerings were introduced? You must also be aware of the presence of any possible nuisance fish and try to work out how to avoid them. I realise that some anglers may consider this a great deal of trouble, but to be consistently successful with extra large fish, there are no short-cuts.

unsatisfactory shine when they are bought. Although this disappears with use, there is a simple way to remove the shine before fishing with them. Put some vinegar into a jam jar and leave the weights and plummets to soak overnight. This will dull their appearance. Then swill them under the cold-water tap, and dry them before placing them in your tackle-box.

Legering Tips

Non-shine leger-weights

Some non-toxic leger-weights and plummets have an

Buoyant lead or feeder link

If you are legering over bottom debris, deep mud or silt, for example, use a buoyant link to ensure that your main line is held clear and is not obstructed.

Take a medium-sized polyball, which has been col-

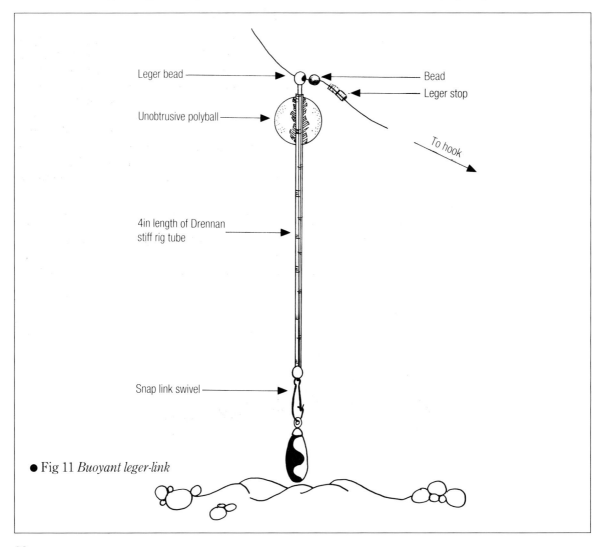

Leger bead

Unobtrusive polyball

4in length of Drennan
stiff rig tube

Snap link swivel

Bead

Leger stop

To hook

● Fig 11 *Buoyant leger-link*

oured with a magic marker to make it inconspicuous, and drill through it a hole of suitable diameter to fit snugly on a 4in length of Drennan stiff rig-tube. Super-glue the polyball adjacent to the end of the tube. Thread a loop of line – as low a breaking strain as you think you can get away with – through the tube (a length of fuse wire used as a needle will facilitate this), looping the line around a leger bead at the polyball end and through a bead and a Drennan snap link at the other. Knot the line and super-glue it for extra security.

This versatile link will now work with a variety of different sized bombs or feeders, which are simply clipped on to the snap link. When you get a take, the line should stay free of the bottom and run through the leger bead with little resistance, which gives more positive bite indication at the rod end. The weak line should break before your main line in the event of the feeder or bomb becoming snagged (see Fig11).

Mounting seed-baits

Rather than mount seed-baits, such as hemp, tares, etc, directly on the hook, thereby risking the hook-point being masked, I prefer to mount them on a version of the hair-rig. A quick and efficient method is as follows.

Slide a short, say ½in, length of rig or Biro tube over the hair, then tie a small dark-coloured polyball on the end of the hair to act as a stop. The polyball will also provide a measure of buoyancy, thereby balancing the weight of the hook and keeping it clear of the bottom. Seed-baits are simply super-glued to the tube, but make

sure that the seeds have been dried carefully first (see Fig12).

In the normal run of events, these tube mounts are rather fiddly to make up on the bank, but it only takes about half-an-hour to make up sufficient at home the night before a fishing trip. I even go so far as to glue on the seeds at home, tying on a new hook complete with seeds when the bait needs changing.

This versatile variation of the hair-rig can also be used with paste baits. The tube prevents soft paste flying off during the cast, and mounting paste like this ensures that the hook point is never masked, even when the paste goes rock-hard in cold water.

Rod-top light

To attach a beta-light or Starlight to the rod-top or quiver-tip for night fishing, simply whip on a length of silicon rubber of suitable diameter as close to the tip ring as possible. Insert the beta-light or Starlight in the tube and manouevre it from side to side so that it sits at right angles to the rod, which makes it easy to see.

A word of warning: don't wet the beta-light to ease entry into the tube because this makes it prone to fly out on the strike. Having to grope around at night trying to find it in fields recently occupied by cows is not recommended!

● Fig 12 *Version of hair-rig for mounting seed or paste baits*

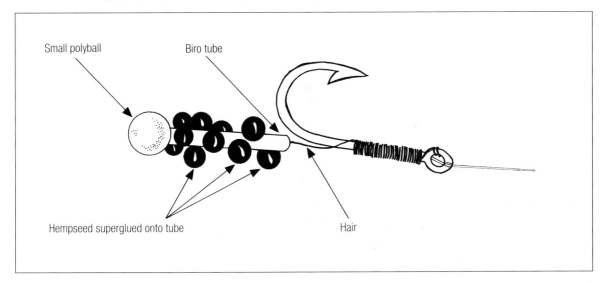

Small polyball   Biro tube

Hempseed superglued onto tube   Hair

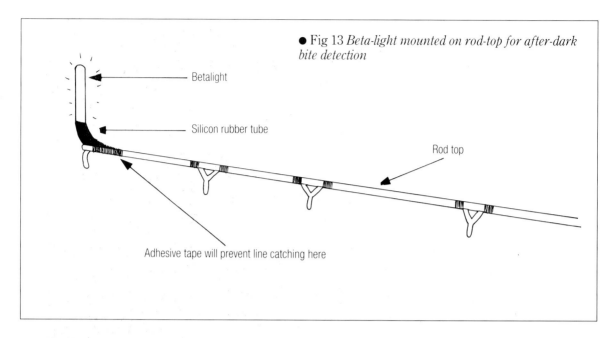

● Fig 13 *Beta-light mounted on rod-top for after-dark bite detection*

Betalight

Silicon rubber tube

Rod top

Adhesive tape will prevent line catching here

A beta-light can either be plugged in or unplugged at will and the silicon rubber will double as a shock-absorber against breakage.

Mug fish

There is a mystery surrounding the fact that some fish are caught any number of times while other members of their group almost always avoid capture. To my knowledge, this phenomenon is true of barbel, carp, chub, tench and pike, and I suspect that it is true of other species.

Jack Hilton's chub of over 7lb from the Royalty is a prime example. Caught twice by Jack himself within an ounce or two of 7lb, and by Bob Buteux the following season at 6lb 7oz, this fish was readily identifiable by three black spots on its gill cover, in addition to its scale arrangement.

A more recent example is a very big barbel, known affectionately as Henrietta. This 14lb 1oz fish, caught in the autumn of 1984 by Greg Buxton, astonished the complete British big-fish fraternity. The capture of this fish assured Greg of his own piece of angling immortality, for he became the first-ever winner of the coveted Drennan Cup competition.

Since that momentous occasion and, indeed, prior to it, Henrietta has gladdened a number of famous barbel angler's hearts. Among these are Pete Reading (14lb

2oz), Bob Moulsely (13lb 8oz) and Martin Hooper (14lb 2oz and 13lb 3oz). Terry Lampard has caught Henrietta on a number of occasions, but unfortunately her heaviest for him was 13lb 11oz.

How do we know, without doubt, that Henrietta has been captured so many times? In fact, Henrietta has two very distinctive features: under her right eye, near the end of a facial line, she has an oval black mark, and the outline of her dorsal fin is quite distinctive. Even if she did not have these marks, we would still be able to recognise her from her scales. A fish's scale arrangement is rather like our fingerprints – each and every one is unique. Of course, fully scaled fish are difficult in the extreme to identify by scale arrangement alone (it is almost impossible to identify tench this way). However, the situation is eased somewhat by the fact that fish have a second set of 'fingerprints' – their fins. The shape, position, colour and number of rays of the fins make identification, if not easy, at least reasonably certain. Other miscellaneous features are facial lines, scars and other injuries, which all aid identification.

● *This Royalty chub was caught twice by Jack Hilton over 7lb. When it was caught later by Bob Buteux, it had slimmed to 6lb 7oz*

● *Bill Quinlan lowers his bait into exactly the right spot*

Good quality photographs are the key to identification, of course, because a detailed examination at the time of capture would put an end to the fish's life.

Theories put forward usually imply that the often caught fish is of a lower intelligence than others in its group; Bob Buteux, for example, christened them 'mug fish'. While it may be true in some instances, it certainly is not true in others. Nevertheless, should Henrietta be considered a mug, I'm one angler who won't complain if she picks up my bait!

8
Roach

by Peter Stone

Roach, or 'red-fins' as they are often called, are the angler's favourite fish. For matchmen roach play an important role, for the pleasure angler a red-fin is always welcome, and the specialist angler, seeking roach, never ceases to be thrilled when a two-pounder slides over his waiting net.

Roach are prolific in the majority of England's rivers and feed in most, if not all, conditions. In the heat of summer I have taken fine catches from under sunken water-lilies, known universally as 'cabbages', and in winter through holes cut in the ice. As you would expect, however, they do feed more freely in certain conditions than in others. The condition of the water is the main factor which decides this – particularly where big roach are concerned – and the roach fisher who is able to recognise the 'right' water condition will fish with that much more confidence. The most favourable conditions and the type of swim to look for I shall discuss later.

Roach of all sizes are taken on both float and leger

● *Peter Stone with a brace of 2-pounders taken from the Evenlode in flood conditions*

● *Peter Stone demonstrates his legering style. From the expression on his face it looks like the roach are not being too co-operative!*

tackle but many anglers find the latter method difficult to master. Most of their difficulties concerns hooking roach bites because this species are very suspicious of resistance, particularly resistance from the rod top.

I first became aware of the problem of resistance in the late 1940s when I became involved in match fishing. At that time rods built specifically for legering were unknown, so I designed and built my own. The main feature of my new legering rod was its extremely fine tip which resulted in a tremendous improvement in my catches – and much silverware decorating my parents' sideboard. (These extra-fine rod tops are now called quiver-tips, of course.) My success was not entirely due to my new rod, however; the position of the line in the water was another, equally important, factor.

When I first started legering seriously for roach, it became apparent that any resistance, both at the rod top and on the line, had ideally to be eliminated. My new

rod more or less solved the rod-top problem, so I concentrated on the line.

Initially, I legered with the bomb/bait lying at right angles – ie, at approximately 90° – to the rod top. Fishing like this, a roach picked up the bait, moved and, feeling the resistance of the rod top, dropped the bait pretty quickly. The answer, I reasoned, was to 'cushion' the resistance to the fish by placing a bow in the line.

On my next visit to the river I experimented by sitting only slightly upstream of where my bait would come to rest, so that with my bait lying on the bottom, the line would be positively and purposely bowed. To my joy, in place of the previous rapid snatches as the roach ejected the bait, slow, easy-to-hit pulls occurred. Almost overnight my roach fishing was transformed.

Much later, I started trout fishing with the wet fly on the River Windrush. All the books I read advised casting across and downstream but warned that takes would be difficult to connect with. My first day was spent striking at snatches with almost no reward. Thinking about it later, it occurred to me that I should cast not downstream and across, as the books recommended, but slightly upstream, thereby ensuring a slight bow formed in the line. The rest is history: in place of mainly unhittable snatches, I got slow pulls which were so easy to hook. Catching trout became almost an embarrassment: it was all due to that small, but vital, bow in the line.

Big rivers

When fishing fairly wide rivers – say, 40yd – and the current speed permits, I try to locate fish either in the middle or towards the far bank so that there is a lot of line in the water. With, say, 20yd of line out and well bowed, bites, most times, will consist of slow pulls which are easy to hook. Fish a shorter line or, worse still, the line at almost right angles to the rod top, much swearing and cursing will result instead of a bag of roach.

After perfecting this method for wide rivers I caught dace – probably the fastest biters around – almost as consistently as roach. Indeed, I can vividly recall winning a match on the Thames, at Appleford, with an all-dace catch taken legering at 30yd range. That win pleased me immensely for, with a big bow in the line, I made what was potentially difficult fishing easy.

Should the current speed permit, a moving bait is more likely to be taken than a stationary one. To achieve this I fish shots, usually SSGs, AAAs and BBs, on a sliding link, adding or removing shots as required. To achieve maximum effect, it is very important that the terminal tackle should roll along the bottom but *only just*. In colder water, however, the roach often prefer a stationary bait.

Regarding terminal tackle, the use of leger stops is widely recommended but most have a tendency to damage, and thereby weaken, especially fine line, and for that reason I don't use them. Split shots are even worse and they have a tendency to slip, resulting in missed bites. Before I stopped using shots I often missed what were confident bites only to find that the shot had slipped down towards the hook. I now prefer to tie my hook links to a small yet strong swivel, with a small bead on the main line above the swivel, between this and the link. This arrangement keeps the link clear of the line, so preventing tangles, and, as an added bonus, the bead protects the knot at the junction between main line and swivel.

Although the rod can be supported in two rests, while legering I don't do it this way. Either I hold the rod supported on one knee or on one rest situated just below the tip. Both ways the rod can be held dead still, which is a very important point. I hold the line either over one or between two fingers as occasions dictate – ie, when bites can be felt more easily than seen.

Another important point is the test-curve of the quiver-tip: this should be chosen so that with the terminal tackle in position the quiver-tip should only be slightly bent; if it is bent over too far, too much resistance will be encountered by the fish as it moves off with the bait. Many rods, including the Drennan Feeder range which I use, carry two quivers of different test-curves; because of their versatility this type is preferable to those with one built in.

The length of rod is a matter of choice, but I like one between 10 and 11½ft. It should, however, be manufactured from one of the latest carbon-fibre composites because this material's light weight, power and casting accuracy adds both to the effectiveness and enjoyment of the technique. A line of 3lb bs should suffice for most situations with a hook link – 18in I find about right for most baits – of 3lb Drennan Double Strength.

Baits

During my match-fishing days, I used bread-paste flavoured with custard powder. As roach love this combination, it will come as no surprise that I still continue to use it today. To make the paste, first cut the crusts from a three-day-old loaf and discard them; then cut the crumb into slices. Hold each piece under a tap for a second and knead the bread into a paste. When you have kneaded several slices, place the crumb in a bowl containing custard powder and knead until the mixture is a brightish yellow. Roach dislike hard paste, so mix until the paste is very soft – so soft, in fact, that it will not stand retrieving. Fred J. Taylor, when he first saw my bread-paste, said 'The roach don't eat your paste, they drink it!' The paste should be kept in a clean rag in a box and out of the sun. It is important, of course, to keep your hands scrupulously clean.

Today, bread-paste has become largely a fogotten bait, mainly, I suspect, because it cannot be bought over the counter. Carp specialists excepted, the majority of anglers cannot be bothered to make their own baits and are missing much as a result.

When fishing bread-paste, I use soaked white breadcrumbs as ground bait, introducing two orange-sized balls at the beginning of the session, with further introductions as and when the roach respond. A word of warning – don't overfeed; as a general rule, one ball every fifteen minutes will suffice. Less, however, should be used in a slow current and only slightly more when the river is flowing more rapidly.

The most popular roach baits are maggots and casters, and not without good reasons – they are readily obtainable and very productive. Maggots, however, tend to encourage and/or attract smaller roach (which I rarely fish for these days), but casters definitely sort out the bigger specimens.

Despite the popularity of maggots, occasions arise when the roach ignore them and I well remember a day when the late great Dick Walker taught me a lesson I will never forget. One bitterly cold January day, Dick and I fished a small Thames tributary and the roach were not responding to our single and double maggot fished under a small float. After a while, Dick announced that he was going 'to sort them out'. Not long after that statement, he started catching. His secret was to use dead maggots. 'In very cold conditions roach often prefer dead maggots,' Dick said, 'so I scalded some before I left home.' That was something new to me, but it certainly worked on that occasion – and on countless other occasions since.

Where extremely big roach are concerned, however, a lobworm cannot be bettered, especially in high coloured water. At such times worms and soil fall into the water and fish are on the lookout. I fish lobworms whole, with a No 8 hook passed through the head once; that way it looks and wriggles in a natural manner.

Marsh worms were highly recommended by Dick Walker and rightly so; brandlings are also good. These worms, two or three together, are fished on a No 14 hook. I usually fish paste on either a No 14 or a No 12 hook, maggots and casters on 18s or 20s. For the latter, the hook link is scaled down to 1.7lb bs, in conjunction with a 2lb bs main line.

When fishing maggots or casters, loose offerings are introduced via an open-ended feeder stuffed with a mixture of maggots/casters and very light crumb. The latter should be packed sufficiently tightly to withstand casting but loose enough so that it disperses as soon as it hits the bottom.

Location

In all fishing situations, location is the most important factor; as Dick Walker tirelessly reminded us. 'You can't catch a fish that isn't there.' This, of course,

applies equally to roach and while in most rivers they are fairly evenly distributed, certain features exist which attract them. One of the most consistent are underwater lilies, or 'cabbages'. Cabbages, however, seem a daunting and formidable prospect to the inexperienced fisherman and are often overlooked by the majority of anglers for this very reason. That is a grave mistake for there are few finer places to find roach, both in numbers and size.

Roach are found among and adjacent to cabbages, mainly, I believe, because of the quantity and variety of insects that inhabit them, and also because in summer they emit oxygen and provide shelter from the sun. But whatever the reason, I seldom pass by a bed of cabbages. They instill confidence in me and confidence is a vital factor in successful fishing – indeed, confidence is often more important than the choice of bait. Although a dense bed of cabbages may look formidable, the secret is to know how to fish them.

If the bed is dense (which does make presentation difficult), take up your position at one end. Tackle up with sufficient shot so that they hold the bottom. Where little or no current is flowing, two SSG shots are sufficient; more must be added if necessary to counteract any flow present.

For convenience, I will assume that the bait is custard-flavoured paste. Attach a No 12 hook to a 3lb bs bottom (I prefer spade-ended hooks, but eyed versions are acceptable) and stop the leger-weight – ie, the shots on the link – some 15in away. Mix some cloud ground bait and introduce two handfuls right against and on the outside of the cabbages. Position yourself so you are level to where the terminal tackle will come to rest.

Cast slightly beyond the cabbages, then as soon as the tackle hits the bottom, pull towards the cabbages until the leger-weight is against them, then tighten gently. There should be a very slight bow in the quiver. On most occasions bites will be positive, the quiver pulling over smartly 3–4in. Sometimes, but certainly not always, a slight indication will occur before the 'pull' proper.

When a roach is hooked, it is a case of 'pull devil, pull

● (inset) *This specimen Dorset Stour chub caught by Tony Arbery is a cracker*

● *Ron Chant with 12lb 14oz of magnificent middle-Avon barbel*

baker', with finesse thrown out of the window. During a successful session, cabbage leaves will float to the surface, having been cut by the line while the fish are being extracted, but it is all part of the fun. When fishing cabbages, I use paste which enables a 3lb bs line to be used. Where the cabbages are particularly dense, I often resort to a 4lb bs line, which is better. The use of maggots and/or casters would probably demand the use of finer tackle, which would undoubtedly result in breakages before the roach were extracted.

Because the bait should be presented right under the cabbages, this method is best suited to conditions in which there is little or no flow. It is also worth remembering that in winter roach are usually found where cabbages were abundant in the summer.

Many anglers miss out considerably by their reluctance to fish in, or close to weed-beds. Countless summer anglers have often told me that the roach did not start feeding until very late in the day. This is balderdash! The much more likely reason was not that the roach were not feeding but that the anglers were fishing in 'open' water, well away from the weeds. As the day progressed, the roach left the weeds because of the increase of carbon dioxide (which fish cannot breathe)

● *Over 32lb of river pike! Caught by Kevin Clifford from a northern river (*Kevin Clifford*)*

● *Portrait of a happy man – Peter displays a beautiful 2lb 10oz roach*

and then fed where the anglers were fishing – ie, the weed-free areas. The angler who wishes to catch roach in the heat of a summer's day must fish where they are – in, or adjacent to, weed-beds.

Methods

Despite the enjoyment I derive from legering, I much prefer float fishing. Fishing a stick float when a slight upstream wind is blowing is great fishing; likewise, when I am fishing the waggler further across the river. Both these methods are well documented in publications and other books, so I do not intend to go into detail here. My intention when invited to pen this chapter was twofold; first, to mention less popular methods of successful roach fishing, and secondly to describe legering in more detail because many anglers still find the technique difficult to master.

Small Stream Fishing

Much of my roach fishing these days takes place on the

Rivers Evenlode and Windrush, close to my home in Oxfordshire. Both of these streams are narrow, with an average depth of 4ft and, in winter, fast flowing. These three factors prevent fishing with a lot of line in the water and sitting almost in line with the bait, which combine to make legering, for roach especially, difficult. For most of the time I am obliged to fish with the line at right angles to the rod, a situation which should be avoided. Also, it is rarely possible to place that all-important bow in the line.

I recall a morning session on the Windrush which went some way to solving my predicament. The river was in roaring flood, the strength of the current pulling my quiver-tip right over. Suddenly the quiver – indeed the rod itself – pulled right round, indicating a typical bite from a big roach in these conditions. I struck and missed. The following four casts in the same spot resulted in four more vicious pulls-round, all of which had me striking at thin air. By this time that 'thin air' around me was very blue indeed. Something had to be done, but what?

On the next cast, as soon as the leger weight touched the bottom, I removed two turns of line from the spool and did not tighten. Seconds later the tip pulled round, this time a little slower, and a further minute later a near 2lb roach was regretting the error of its ways. By removing those two turns of the line I was able to place a little, but vitally important, bit of slack line between the rod top and weight, which helped to cushion the pull.

Nowadays, having selected a swim, I position myself as far away from it, within reason, as possible – say, 30ft. As soon as the terminal tackle hits the bottom, two or three turns of the line are removed from the spool. I then, very gently tighten to the quiver. With the rod top close to the water there is now a little slack between the quiver and the weight. Bites, as a rule, result in the quiver-tip pulling quite rapidly round, by sometimes as much as 6in. Most, however, are still missed and much swearing takes place! But when conditions/situations dictate that legering must be resorted to, which is most of the time on these two rivers, I cannot think of anything else to make the fishing any easier. It is most frustrating, especially on the Evenlode, knowing that big roach are picking up the bait but not swallowing it, merely holding it between their lips, because of too much resistance.

My biggest roach from the Evenlode weighed 2lb 15oz. It picked up a piece of crust as the light was fading (the very best time for roach, I find). The bite was no more than a minute pull on the quiver. Small bites are the ones I like best because the roach is confident and has swallowed the bait, obviously making it easier to hit. Unfortunately, they occur far less often than the big pulls, which are much more likely to be missed. One way to overcome the problem is to leger upstream. This is a neglected method, yet practised in the right place one that can be very successful.

Having positioned yourself well downstream of the swim, a weight is chosen which will hold the bottom, but only just – that is very important. As the terminal tackle touches the bottom, take up any slack line and hold the rod with the tip pointing upwards. Bites are detected by watching the line, which will drop back towards you as soon as the fish moves off with the bait. Generally speaking, the majority of bites will be successfully hooked simply because a minimum of resistance is felt by the fish which, in consequence, takes the bait firmly into its mouth.

In summer, many small streams have prolific beds of ranunculus, sometimes referred to as streamer weed, under which roach (and other species) like to lie. Here a bait fished right under or alongside the weed stands an excellent chance of being taken. In place of shots on a sliding link, I prefer to use an Arlesey bomb in this situation because it 'cuts' through the weed more readily.

I have already discussed some of the problems when legering in small streams and undoubtedly there are others. One answer is to use a float. The way in which a bait is presented under a float, however, depends upon the size of the roach expected, or preferred.

For roach up to, say, 1lb in weight, trotting is the best method. For this a stick float cannot be bettered the bait being either small fragments of breadcrust, maggot or caster. A 1.7lb bs line will give excellent presentation, and the angler must keep a low profile to prevent scaring the fish.

For bigger roach, however, I prefer laying on. Today, this is a very neglected method, which I find strange for one simple reason: at no time does the fish encounter anything but the minimum of resistance. A float, similar to a waggler, is attached to the line at the top and bottom (double rubber), the shots bunched, say 15in, from the hook. (For crust, this distance will be 4in.) After the depth of the swim has been ascertained (by means of a small plummet), the float is pushed up the line a further 4in. (In other words, it is now 4in overdepth.)

When the bait is in position, the line is gently tightened to the float until it rides the surface at 'half-cock'. The rod is either held or supported in a pair of rests, with the line taut to the float and completely clear of the water. Most times when a bite occurs the float will rise almost vertically before gently sliding under the water. Sometimes it will not rise but simply travel sideways, sometimes sinking as it does, sometimes not; or it may suddenly drop flat.

Laying on is my favourite method for catching roach with a float. In winter, when roach tend to move around less, it is especially effective. When fishing lobworms, because of the almost complete lack of resistance, plenty of time can be allowed for the roach to take the bait right into its mouth.

One of the delights of roach fishing is that they feed all day, even in the hottest weather. Where big roach in small shallow rivers are concerned, however, this does not apply, because big roach do not like bright light. My long experience seeking big roach has shown, beyond any doubt, that dawn, the last hour of daylight and night-time are best. This applies both in summer and winter. The exception is in coloured water which reduces the amount of light entering it.

● *'Old Stoney' won a Drennan Cup award for this 2lb 15oz monster from the Evenlode*

The majority of the 2lb-plus roach that I have taken in daylight have come from coloured water. When the rivers are in flood or, more precisely, just beginning to drop, I make every effort to fish for I know my chances are then excellent.

In the winter of 1991–2 my regular angling companion, Geoff Barnes, awoke to find the River Evenlode (which flows alongside his home) in flood. He phoned me but work unfortunately prevented me from joining him. Geoff decided to get down to the river immediately but was delayed and arrived two hours later than he had intended. The swim Geoff had in mind fishes extremely well in such conditions, so he was dismayed as he approached to see that another angler was already fishing there. The angler had arrived only an hour before Geoff and had already caught a monster roach. It was caught on his second cast of the day and weighed no less than 3lb 2oz! The delay, without doubt, had cost Geoff that fish.

A few weeks earlier, a match on the same water had

been won with four roach, three of them well over 2lb each, the other only a fraction under. That day the river was also running high and coloured, the fish being taken on the edge of slack water. It was a tremendous catch, but that is not the end of the story. When the scalesman asked the angler what he had caught, the reply was 'Four bream'. When it was pointed out to him that they were roach, he replied, 'I did not know roach grew that big.' Often in rivers in the right conditions big roach can become almost suicidal and easy to catch as a result (like those in the reach of the Evenlode in question). This is very far from the usual case, where most days they are extremely difficult and only occasionally caught.

A factor which makes many anglers more successful than others is being able to 'read the water', thus being able to recognise the type of swim likely to hold the fish they seek. Many writers have recommended slacks and eddies for big roach but, with the exception of high coloured water, I do not agree. The trouble with slacks

● *A 2lb 8oz roach from the Evenlode, taken with the rain falling and in poor light – excellent conditions for big roach*

and eddies is that they usually contain rubbish washed down by the strong currents, making presentation always difficult and, at times, almost impossible. Also, roach do not always favour such places, particularly those in which the water surface 'boils'. Having said that, a slack and/or eddy where the bottom is clean is always worth trying, and the area where slack adjoins the main flow is often the best place.

In my experience, the best roach swims are where the water flows evenly over a gravel bottom. The speed of the current is not important; roach are not deterred by fast water, but they do like an evenly paced current. Such swims need not be deep either; I catch many big roach in swims no more than 3ft deep, and sometimes less than that.

Another favourite haunt of roach are bulrushes (often referred to as 'onions' or 'pipes'). Bulrushes only grow on gravel and roach love both the gravel and the shade and sanctuary that the bulrushes provide.

Weir-pools can be fished effectively both with float and leger, but usually with the latter. A method which involves the use of a float, and a bait used only by a small minority of anglers, is trotting with silk-weed. I first used this method some fifty years ago, and where silk-weed is still found on weir-sills, it can be used to

great effect even today. The soft, dense weed contains masses of different insects upon which roach (and not discounting other species) feed. Having tackled up with a 3lb bs line and an AAA shot-loading float (attached top and bottom), the shots are bunched some 18in from the hook – a No 10. It is important that when the weed is placed on the hook, the hook should be drawn through the weed which should not be touched by your fingers. Why the fish should ignore the weed if it has been touched is difficult to understand, but I have always found it to be so. The float is set some 3ft from the hook, then it is cast into the top of the white water and allowed to travel downstream without hindrance. Bites consist of the float going straight under or travelling sideways – a largely forgotten method but a very successful one.

The methods I have described are not the be-all and end-all of roach fishing, but those I have used with great success during the course of the past fifty years or so. There are others which I have used much less but I never write about methods/baits that I am not fully conversant with.

At the beginning of this chapter I said that roach are the most popular of all coarse fish, and few anglers would surely argue with that. I am often asked what is

● *Another 2-pounder taken in bright sunshine but the river heavily coloured with floodwater*

my favourite fish, but that is a question I cannot answer. However, of all the big fish of many species that have graced my net over the years, nothing excites me more than when a 2lb roach surfaces on the end of my line. It may be no more than 14–15in in length, but what a big fish it undoubtedly is.

I will let the doyen of roach fishers, the late Ted Ensom (Faddist) have the final word of this piece:

The roach fisherman must be prepared to serve a reasonable apprenticeship before achieving an all-round competency. There is no short-cut. Persistence, thoroughness, patience and common-sense application are the essential keys. None of our fresh-water fish is sought after so assiduously, and by so many anglers, as the roach. The roach is the common quest. It is a boon and a blessing to Mr Everyman angler.

Which is where I came in. Best of luck to you all.

9
Pike Fishing

Because I uphold the popular opinion that summer pike are not as fit, and therefore not as hard fighting, as their winter counterparts, I only fish for them in the colder months. Even very cold water will not prevent pike feeding, though, I suppose, a temperature over 38°F is preferable. So, as long as the water is not too coloured, river pike may be relied upon to provide unrivalled winter sport. And I am not talking only about average-sized pike, because rivers have produced many big fish, including several 30-pounders, in recent years, with, perhaps, overcast conditions proving best for producing the biggest fish of all.

The above makes it difficult to explain or understand why pike fishing is largely neglected by the majority of river anglers in the wintertime. Of course, there are pike anglers on the riverbank throughout the colder months, but most appear to ignore the fact that they are fishing a river and try to treat it as just another stillwater. Their first priority seems to be to find a largish pool, preferably with little or no flow so that tackle control is relatively straightforward. Here they deposit a mountain of tackle, cast out, erect their umbrella and remain all day until it is time to pack up. I suppose this method must work to some extent because so many anglers persevere with it weekend after weekend, but in most instances it is far from the best plan.

The first thing to appreciate is that although river-pike fishing is a very different game from that practised on stillwaters, it is no more difficult. In fact, long casting, for example, is rarely necessary. You can use the currents to carry your tackle to the desired spot and into places where it would be impossible to cast. And much more successful, and far more enjoyable, is a roving approach. The feeling of eager anticipation as you travel along the river, fishing every likely spot, is intensely exciting.

Another possible reason for river-pike fishing's lack of popularity is that it is very much a solitary affair. Sharing the fishing with a companion reduces effective-ness for two main reasons. First, it costs time; discussing the fishing may be of some value, but a winter's day is very short and river piking entails a lot of non-fishing time while you move about. When alone, you are your own master, free to roam when and where you will, perhaps to another stretch or even to another river. Secondly, fishing in company cuts your chances; in any given stretch there are only so many swims and only so many pike, so you and your friends are fishing for the same fish. Of course, this is a selfish attitude, but there is more to it than that. When fishing alone, you are absolutely quiet and as a result you can concentrate better and fish more effectively. However, should you feel it necessary to pike fish with a companion, where possible take one bank each. Fishing that way you get almost the best of both worlds. Fishing from a boat is the exception, because handling a boat in tricky currents, etc, is easier and safer when you are accompanied by an experienced companion.

Location

In faster stretches, most pike swims will be close to the banks, but this does not mean that fast shallows in mid-river should be neglected – in fact, some river pikers recommend that these are the most productive places. That is not my experience, however, where very big fish are concerned. River pike don't seem to like water that is too deep – depths of between 3ft and 8ft are perhaps the best.

My own particular favourite pike swims include the inside of bends; deepish pools adjacent to flood rafts, and the crease formed between slack and faster water. The water under overhanging trees and bushes is also

---

● *A large Stour pike is given the butt by Jack Hilton*

well worth trying, as is anywhere where tree roots, fallen trees or other debris provide a lair for the pike. Downstream of anything that diverts the flow, such as where the bank juts out into the river, as long as the depth is suitable, is yet another good area, as is an area close to where the weeds stay green throughout the year and adjacent to rush- or reed-beds.

Most reliable pike swims are also reliable for other species – for example, dace and roach. This is hardly surprising, for pike won't be far away from their prey; they, too, don't want to work any harder than necessary for their food. Of course, you can put this information to good use by trying to keep and/or to attract small prey fish to your pike swim(s). This is an important, yet often overlooked, aspect of pike fishing. Therefore, make room in your pike-tackle carrier to take some maggots and/or ground-bait with you. It is also advisable to keep some reserves in the car in case you need them. The last thing you want is to run out on the day: ground-bait is *the* vital component.

Feed your pike swims just as you would when you are fishing for dace or roach. The more fodder fish you can attract and keep in the swim, the better your chances of attracting, and ultimately catching, pike.

I have been reminded by Bob James of another area well worth the trouble of more than cursory attention, especially later in the season. At this time of year, dace, particularly, leave the main river to spawn. Often the spawning grounds, preferred by dace, etc, are in streams or carriers that are too shallow for pike to negotiate. Unable to follow the dace, the pike do the next best thing – lay in ambush, awaiting the return of their food fish. Therefore, search carefully any likely areas for pike close to any stream's mouth, no matter how insignificant the stream may appear, because the pike will be waiting there, as close as conditions allow, for an easy meal. The consistently successful pike angler always endeavours to provide it.

Tackle

The following important guidelines were given by Max Cottis in the *Coarse Fisherman* magazine's supplement, *Pike '90*.

The first thing you must do when you decide to go pike fishing is to choose the right tackle. All too often

I see people using rods designed for other purposes being grossly overloaded with the combined weight of bait and rig. The result is that the angler can't cast any distance and when he hooks a fish, the rod doesn't have enough backbone to offer any sort of control. This situation often leads to lost fish, sometimes still carrying the angler's tackle, a situation that clearly is not good for pike.

The roving pike angler must travel light: two rods, at most (already set up), a landing-net, a small tackle-carrier, a folding stool and baits still sounds a lot to carry, but it can be done easily. If you carry the tackle-box over your shoulder and the stool around your neck both your hands are left free, one to carry your rod(s) and the other for your landing-net and live-bait bucket.

Each and every item of tackle, no matter how insignificant it at first might seem, must be considered carefully. The live-bait bucket is no exception. Mine started its working life as a container for 15 litres of ice-cream. It was chosen mainly because of its tight-fitting lid. I have two lids: one is unadulterated and used during travelling so that river water does not spill into the car; the other lid has been perforated with lots of $\frac{1}{4}$in diameter holes. This second lid enables the bucket, complete with baits, to be submerged in the river. The holes provide good water transference without allowing the baits to escape. Retaining baits in this manner ensures that they are not damaged and are kept in tip-top condition. This is especially important when you are on an extended trip. On such occasions the bucket is kept submerged in the river overnight, in addition to every possible opportunity during the day.

The reliable, undoubtedly effective and refined pike tackle that is available today is largely due to many thinking (and caring) anglers, in addition to the tackle manufacturers. Companies such as E. T. Products, Middy and Drennan, to name but three in the field, have all developed gear, especially terminal tackle, which leaves little to be desired. And there is no excuse these days to use inferior hooks, unreliable trace wire and swivels, etc. Always use the best tackle and you will keep lost fish down to a minimum. This can only be good for you and the pike.

Pike rods

Should you decide to fish the rivers for pike and you are serious and conscientious, you should purchase rod(s)

● A wobbled dead-bait is tried by Bill Keal

that are designed for the job. They need not be very expensive, for companies like DAM, Silstar, Ryobi and Shakespeare, among others, produce budget-priced pike rods. If you cannot even aspire to one such as these, please don't fish for pike.

Usually, longish rods are more versatile on rivers for various reasons and my own choice is for a length of around 12ft. The exceptions are when you are fishing from a boat or on a small stream, when shorter rods can be handled more easily. Two rods are customary, one set up for float fishing, the other for legering. Pike rods, more than others, need to be robustly built because they

must withstand very hard use and abuse. All my rods were made by Drennan.

An inexpensive rod for handling lures of all types and sizes is the Spinflex, which is designed for spinning with a fixed-spool reel, the style beloved by many practitioners of the art in Britain. The 18in long cork handle is comfortable and will remain firm in your grip in icy conditions. Its action is light and responsive with a flick-tip which enables plugs and spinners to be cast with pin-point accuracy, and also allows the angler to feel exactly how the lure is working during the retrieve. The Spinflex also boasts an enormous reserve of hidden power, which comes in high up on the middle and top sections in a progressive manner. This provides both excellent big-fish control and enjoyable playing of even small fish. The makers recommend line strengths between 5lb–12lb, although I use 14lb Specimen Plus on mine. But always remember to angle the rod *toward* the fish when exerting maximum pressure, otherwise you risk breaking the rod; obviously, this applies whatever rod is in use.

The excellent balance of the Drennan 12ft Pike Float rod allows this powerful 2–2¼lb test-curve rod to be held for long periods without fatigue. This balance, combined with extra length, helps to achieve a perfect line and float control. This rod is particularly important on rivers, especially when fishing far bank swims.

Constructed from extra power 100 per cent spiral graphite, complete with Fuji rings, the 12ft Pike Float rod has a false handle which ferrules in below the FPS reel fitting, thus retaining the action of a two-piece 12ft rod, while providing a maximum joint length of 5ft 4in.

Of similar construction but providing even more power is the 2½lb test-curve, 12ft Pike Dead-bait rod. This rod is designed to cope with a wide range of dead-baits and provides excellent fishing/playing characteristics. This 'meaty' rod has plenty of tip power to cast big baits and set hooks at a distance, even in deep and swiftly flowing swims.

Reels

My choice of reel for river pike is the Shimano Gt4000 Aero Bait-runner, or, besides being made to exacting standards and as near as possible tangle-free, they have one more major advantage over other fixed-spool reels. Using the Aero Bait-runner means that you can dispense with additional audible alarms because, should your attention waver, the sound of the bait-runner will alert you to a taking fish. In addition, there is the weight-saving advantage – an important consideration to the roving angler, for you don't want to carry any more than you have to.

Line

Constant casting and retrieving, pulling out of weed-beds and snags, and fishing in tight situations, with the ever-present danger of getting hung up, is punishing on the line, so my main line is never lower than 14lb bs. It isn't worth taking the chance of snapping off using anything less. In desperate 'do-or-die' swims, I may even resort to 20lb bs. Drennan Specimen Plus, besides being reliable, will withstand much abuse and, therefore, is my choice which I unreservedly recommend.

Method

Where conditions allow, I generally fish two rods simultaneously in each swim. The leger rod is armed with

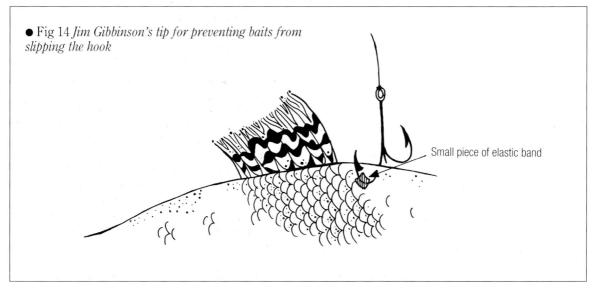

● Fig 14 *Jim Gibbinson's tip for preventing baits from slipping the hook*

Small piece of elastic band

nothing more sophisticated than two size 8, semi-barbless trebles, on an 18in long wire trace. A bomb of around 3oz holds the bait securely in position in most swims, but this is not the only reason for such a heavy weight. It allows me to know immediately when a pike has taken the bait and ensures that 'drop-back' bites are not possible. Drop-back bites would not be indicated by the bait-runner, of course.

The bait on this leger rod is usually a sardine, but use fresh sardines from the fishmongers, not the tinned variety. Fresh sardines have fairly firm flesh and emit a strong oily flavour, which carries well in water. I am sure that pike can detect this attractive oily flavour from some distance away and they use it to home in on the bait.

I strike as soon as the bait-runner announces its warning. Any delay could be fatal, either because the pike has swallowed the bait, resulting in deep hooking, or because it has dropped the bait. An immediate strike is, therefore, better from both the angler's point of view and for the fish's welfare.

My second rod is set up in a similar fashion, the only difference being the addition of a sliding-float, and a lighter weight rests immediately above the trace. Baits are mounted on the trebles by hooking the end hook through the pectoral fin and the upper hook just forward of the dorsal fin. In his book *Modern Specimen Hunting*, Jim Gibbinson passes on a tip to prevent baits from coming adrift during use. After mounting the bait, a small piece of elastic band is impaled on the hook point and beyond the barb. This, of course, stops the hook from coming out. It is simple, yet so effective (see Fig 14).

Boat-fishing Safety

Initially, I had not intended to discuss the necessity of wearing life-preservers when afloat. However, when recently discussing safety in boats, many anglers argued that the risks are negligible. Clearly, this 'head-in-the-sand' attitude is a mistaken belief, for it has been grimly illustrated in recent years that safety is of paramount importance and must be the first consideration of each and every angler who takes to a boat. It is a sad but undeniable fact that each year sees tragic boating accidents in which anglers lose their lives, and many more than most people are aware of. Simply because you don't hear about these accidents does not mean that they do not occur, and they don't all necessarily involve the inexperienced and/or foolhardy anglers.

Bill Quinlan and two companions were fishing a Thames weir-pool from one of the most stable boats on the river, a large Thames punt. They did not see a fallen tree being carried by the current until it hit the punt, which capsized, throwing all three anglers into the swirling water. Bill was the only one wearing a life-jacket and, despite putting his own life at risk, managed to save one of his companions. Even though he was a strong swimmer, the other angler drowned.

Last summer, on the placid waters of Queenford Lagoon, one of Britain's top big-fish men, Andy Mundy, fell from his boat while he was occupied in the seemingly simple task of baiting his swim. Despite witnessing the incident and frantically rushing to the spot, a friend arrived too late to save Andy. Police divers recovered his body the following day.

Kevin Clifford considers himself very lucky to have escaped with his life after a similar incident at a reservoir. Being a strong swimmer, he did not panic, yet if someone had not had the presence of mind to dive in to help, Kevin believes that he would have drowned. Kevin admits that he made mistakes: first, he was not wearing a life-jacket; secondly, he did not remove enough of his clothes – the pockets of his Barbour jacket filled with water and acted as effective drogues; thirdly, he did not appreciate how quickly his energy would drain – the period of time between the first signs of tiredness and complete exhaustion was so brief, that it was almost instantaneous.

These tragedies, possible tragedies and other incidents like them, could be avoided by the simple expedient of wearing a life-preserver. It is not necessary to wear a bright orange life-jacket, although there is nothing wrong with these. A Crew Saver, for example, is worn unobtrusively around the neck like a scarf. In the event of the wearer ending up in the water, the Crew Saver inflates automatically and keeps the victim's head above the water, even if the wearer has been rendered unconscious. Before taking to a boat again, I shall certainly wear a life-preserver of this type.

Anybody who ventures out in a boat, especially on to a swiftly flowing, wind-swept river, in wintertime, without wearing a life-preserver, can only be considered extremely foolish. (More essential safety advice and survival techniques will be found in *Freshwater Fishing* by Hugh Falkus and Fred Buller.)

Techniques

On big wide rivers where strong tides don't make it impossible to control the boat and/or tackle, trolling (or more correctly, trailing) might at first be considered an extremely effective method. This is not my experience. By the very nature of trolling, a wide area of water is covered, which is all very well in very deep, relatively snag-free waters. Unfortunately, big pike in the rivers I fish don't frequent or, more accurately, don't frequently feed in such places. They are more likely to be found in areas such as those listed above, so river-pike techniques, as practised by my friends and myself, are very similar whether we are fishing from the bank or boat. But don't become a slave to one favoured, productive method. Keep an open mind and try to have a flexible outlook. I have lost count of how many times a change from a fancied method has turned up trumps.

Float-fished paternoster

(Please refer to Figs 15 and 16, which are largely self-explanatory.)

Adjustment to the length of the tail keeps the bait working at the desired depth (in most deep swims, two-thirds depth is about right to start with). If you get no response, a different setting may prove effective. In fact, on occasions when no takes are forthcoming at any other depth, it seems that you can elicit a response by fishing almost on the bottom. Mick Brown suggests that you actually knock the pike and, in so doing, stir them into action. The tail, of course, needs to be fashioned from a much lower breaking strain than the main tackle. Then, in the event of the bomb snagging, only this is lost, without undue strain on the reel-line.

Relatively long casts – for example, when you are fishing opposite-bank swims – necessitates keeping as much line as possible off the water, otherwise the tackle will soon be dragged out of position. To do this, you must stand and hold the rod as high as comfort will allow. As it is so fatiguing, you won't be able to do it for long periods, but its effectiveness can be well worth the discomfort. Using the smallest baits will aid tackle control in such circumstances.

● *Roger Smith and Peter Frost record the measurements of a specimen Dorset Stour pike*

In very turbulent waters, such as weir-pools, tackle control can be most difficult. If you feel that the float is more of a hindrance than a help, dispense with it. Takes will still be obvious so long as you keep your mind on the job in hand.

Wire placed between the bait and the link needs to be kept short – never more than a foot. In conjunction with the heavy lead, this prevents the bait from sprinting to a refuge when a pike approaches. At this time the last thing you want is for the bait to get hung up.

When using the float-fished paternoster in a large swim, start at the upstream end. Leave the bait in position for four or five minutes, then, by lifting the rod, raise the tackle, walk a few steps downstream before allowing the bomb to settle once more. Repeat until the downstream end of the swim is reached. In a particularly big swim, it may be best to repeat this procedure more than once and to fish different lines. I would start by fishing very close to the bank; my long rods allow me to stay far enough back not to frighten the fish, my second line being, say, a rod-length out, and so on.

Sink-and-draw or wobbling

The basic idea behind the sink-and-draw method (alternatively called wobbling) is to use a dead-bait in such a manner as to simulate the movements of a live fish. The method is more productive and, to my opinion, more interesting, than waiting for a dead-bait to be picked up from off the bottom. Although static dead-bait fishing can produce on days when nothing else does, it is a method that does not inspire me with confidence. I prefer, therefore, to try sink-and-draw tactics before resorting to a static dead-bait. Also, by trying a few passes with a wobbled dead-bait first, you can learn the vagaries of a new swim before chancing one of your few precious live-baits.

Of course, sink-and-draw tactics must be considered as much more than just an alternative method where live-baiting is not permitted or when live-baits are not available. A wobbled dead-bait can be manoeuvred to cover areas that are impossible or impractical to fish with live-baits. Close to snags, under overhanging bushes, or narrow runs between weed-beds are obvious instances. In areas where depth fluctuates, sink-and-draw may be *the* method. By altering the speed of the retrieve and/or the angle of the rod, a wobbled dead-bait can be lowered into deep holes and raised to skip over shallows at will. It can also be worked into every nook

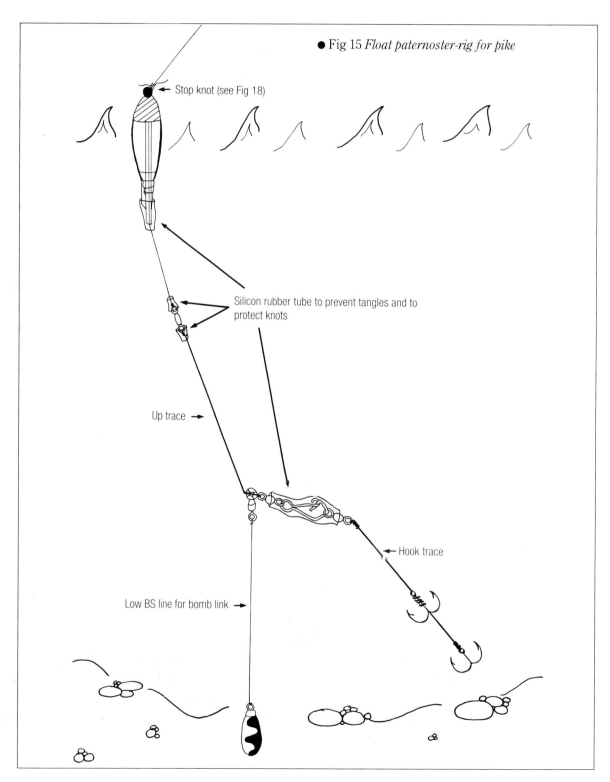

● Fig 15 *Float paternoster-rig for pike*

Stop knot (see Fig 18)

Silicon rubber tube to prevent tangles and to protect knots

Up trace →

Low BS line for bomb link →

← Hook trace

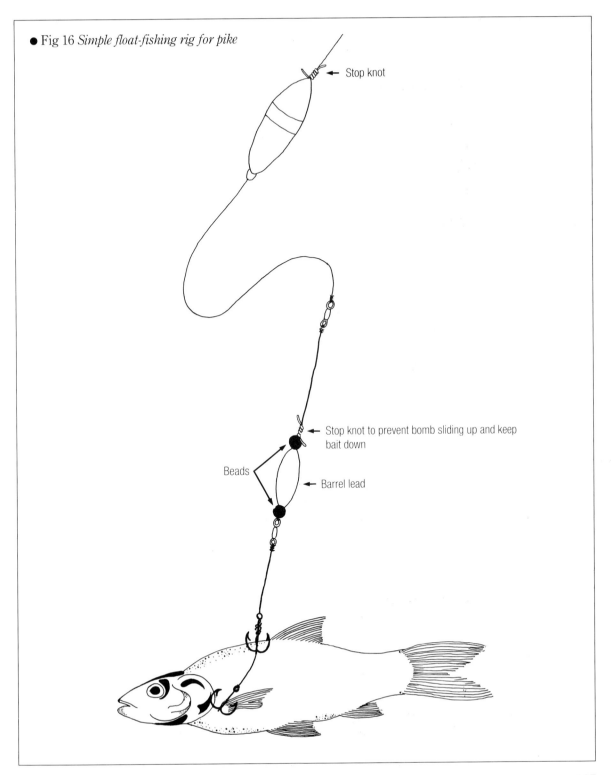

● Fig 16 *Simple float-fishing rig for pike*

← Stop knot

← Stop knot to prevent bomb sliding up and keep bait down

Beads

← Barrel lead

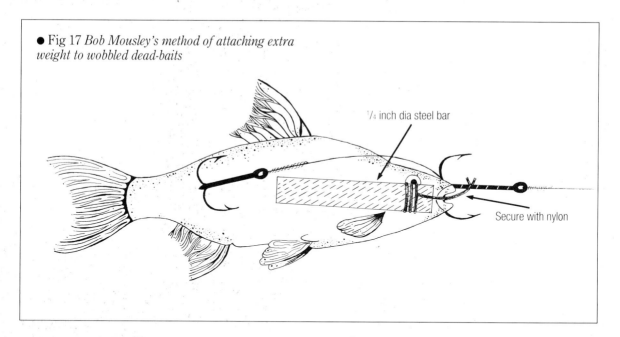

● Fig 17 *Bob Mousley's method of attaching extra weight to wobbled dead-baits*

¹/₄ inch dia steel bar

Secure with nylon

and cranny, searching out pike in otherwise inaccessible areas.

Bait size is not too important, but for most situations one of around 4oz will prove the most convenient.

In that important work, *Pike: The Predator Becomes the Prey* by John Bailey and Martyn Page, Bob Mousley, in his chapter on Wessex rivers, introduced me to the best way yet tried of adding additional weight to wobbled dead-baits. Bob recommends an alternative to lead weights, because this will remove the ever-present danger to pike of a lingering death from lead-poisoning after they have ingested a lost bait. Bob suggests ¼in diameter mild steel between 1½–3in long, depending on the current strength and depth (these sizes have sufficed for me).

In use, tie a 6in length of nylon around one end of a bar and push the other end down the bait's throat until the tied end is in its mouth. Pass the top treble of a two-treble trace through both lips, and tie the two ends of the nylon around the shank. Should the bait be lost, the weight will be retained (see Fig 17).

Where necessary, a float may be incorporated to add another dimension to sink-and-draw tactics. The float needs to be streamlined (see below) and fished over-depth. My choice of float is a large Drennan Zippler, fixed fairly tightly on the line so that it can be moved only by firm pressure. You don't want it to move while you are casting, but you do need to adjust it to fish

swims of differing depths. Also, a degree of movement may save the day in the unlikely event of the float becoming entangled in weeds or a snag. A stop-knot, tied from power-gum and in conjunction with a bead, is employed as the top fixing and a piece of tight-fitting silicon-rubber tube is applied at the bottom. These fixings have been chosen carefully for, coupled with the streamlined shape, they allow the float to pass relatively easily through weed-beds without continually getting hung up. And using a streamlined float ensures that there is less chance of a pike mistaking it for a bait.

When trotting down, hold back so that the bait rises clear of the bottom. Periodically, by releasing the line, let the bait sink to the bottom, then trap the line and raise the rod to get the bait to rise to the surface. Retrieve as slowly as possible, bringing the bait back upstream close to the bank. Takes can come at any time and, even though you are half-expecting it to happen, they will often shock you with their suddenness.

Because big plugs and spinners are so expensive (I no longer make my own), and even though they can be very effective, I rarely use one, so I don't feel qualified to pass any comment.

● *The end result: Alec Lewis contemplates a mean-looking pike*

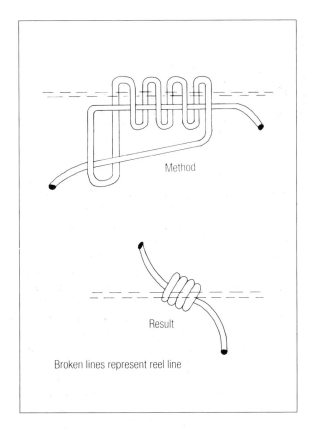

Method

Result

Broken lines represent reel line

● Fig 18 *Power-gum stop-knot*

Unhooking

Undoubtedly the most potentially dangerous period in a pike's life is the time that it spends as our captive, and we must take every care to protect its well being. A landing-net is far preferable to that out-dated implement the gaff. Even in skilled hands, a gaff has been known to inflict horrendous injuries, and not only to the pike. Remember, the pike you catch today are only there because they were previously handled carefully and correctly.

Ensure that the landed fish is laid on something soft; the bottom of a boat should be covered in thick carpet or something similar. On the bank, an unhooking mat is preferable to soft grassy places because, even if the latter is soft, it is still too hard. Firmly restrain the fish to prevent it damaging itself, but don't grip it so tightly that its scales are removed. Try to get the pike out of the landing-net before it tangles the whole thing in knots and wait until it calms down before unhooking.

Unhooking equipment should include a few specialised tools: strong and thick-nosed long-handled forceps; standard long-nosed forceps; long-handled wire-cutters, and a strong leather glove to protect your hand while you insert your fingers under the chin (with the pike tummy upwards, lift the head and the mouth will open automatically).

Hook removal is made much easier by using barbless or flattened barbed hooks, by using the smallest practical size of treble (rarely larger than size 8), and by using not more than two hooks per rig. Hooks lodged in the mouth are eased out with forceps and really need no further explanation. For deeper-set hooks, I fully concur with what Neville Fickling said in the *Coarse Fisherman* magazine's *Pike '90* supplement:

The pike's mouth is held open by inserting a gloved finger under the chin and the trace pulled until the trace is fully revealed. The hooks should appear and can be inverted via the gill covers so as to allow the hooks to pop clear. The second hook should then follow and be removed using the same procedure. I honestly do not feel that a description in print really helps all that much. If in doubt, try to go out with an experienced pike angler, as that is the best way to learn.

I recommend any budding pike angler to join the Pike Anglers' Club – most of the top pikers in Great Britain are members. All those who are interested in pike are welcome and there are regular teach-ins, etc, from which even the experienced have gained benefit.

10
Care of Big Fish

From fellow big-fish man, Dave Ball, came some sickening news recently: the 14lb barbel caught by me in March 1990, and one of the few barbel of record potential, had been found dead shortly after being caught for the last time. The devastating pain from the impact of this news was not eased when I realised that perhaps some of the blame for this sad event must lay with me. Although it had been caught at least twice more after I had taken it, perhaps the publicity I gave it, even though the river was not named and I took great pains to conceal the background in the photographs, inadvertently gave away the fish's whereabouts. But what is the alternative? Every angler I know enjoys reading about the capture of big fish in the fishing papers and magazines. If no big fish were ever reported, many anglers would be bereft of this enjoyment and sales of fishing journals would plummet, so depriving some people of their livelihood. Therefore, the answer to the question posed must be education: education on how to care for our quarry, particularly for the fighting and forever game barbel.

However, before this piece is construed as a personal attack on anyone in particular, let me tell you how another fine barbel almost died by my hand alone.

In the early 1980s I was fishing, of necessity, a short afternoon/evening session on my own for midwinter barbel. Right on dusk, a 6lb barbel was landed and returned. Even so, my instincts led me to believe that I was not in the right place, so, without even trying another cast, I moved 20yd or so upstream. On my first cast in the new swim, a barbel was hooked and lost. On the next cast, I broke on the strike. Even as I reached into my box for my torch to retackle, I thought that I had wasted my two good chances.

I then realised that I had either left my torch at home or lost it. However, years of practice had taught me how to tie up in the dark, although, of course, it would take longer – time that could be ill-afforded. Eventually, everything was ready and on the very next cast another

big barbel was hooked. I could hardly believe my good fortune. I made no mistakes this time, and after a titanic struggle in the dark, a 10lb 3oz barbel was landed.

Although time was short and it had started to rain, I reckoned that if I was quick, there was just sufficient time for a picture or two. So I sacked up the barbel hurriedly while I got my camera ready. The camera on its tripod was placed under my umbrella and my tackle-box acted as a marker where the fish would eventually be held. Because I lacked a torch, correct focusing was achieved by placing a beta-light in a hunk of bread on top of my box and focusing the camera on the beta-light. When all was ready, I went to fetch the fish.

It was gone! In all the excitement and bustle I had forgotten to tie the sack securely to the rod-rest. In blind panic, I rushed downstream hoping to find the sack. I saw, despite the gloom, what I thought was the sack, but without my landing-net, it was too far out in the river to reach. Back I raced to the swim to collect my net but, by the time I returned to where I thought I had seen the sack, it had disappeared once more. I walked further and further downstream, until once more through the darkness and the drizzle, with great good fortune, I spotted the sack. With the first scoop of the landing-net, the sack, complete with barbel, was retrieved.

I am not considered emotional by most who know me, yet I cried with relief at that moment. During the previous half-hour or so I had experienced the full range of emotions. First the euphoria of catching a specimen barbel; then the depths of despair when I believed that I had sentenced that fine fish to a lingering death from starvation, imprisoned in my sack; finally, the surge of relief that swept through me when the situation was retrieved. I don't ever want to go through anything like that again! Perhaps it is now not so difficult to understand why all the pictures taken that night were hopeless – the best showing only half of a double-figure barbel.

From the foregoing you can see that you can never be

too careful. I have prided myself that during the twenty-five years that I have been a barbel-fishing enthusiast, I have never lost a fish through bad management or bad handling – a proud record that was almost destroyed on the evening described.

In summer, especially at times of low water, the amount of dissolved oxygen in the river water is low also. If it has been hot and windless, this condition will be compounded, of course. Towards the end of August 1990, when 'my' big barbel was caught for the final time, the river was very low, the stream almost non-existent, and the water temperature was high. Obviously, the dissolved oxygen content was also low.

We all know that fish require oxygen as vitally as any air-breathing creature. And, after undue exertion, not to mention stress, this requirement increases dramatically. A poor fight from a river fish in summer can indicate that dissolved oxygen levels are low, for if there is a lack of oxygen available, the fish will display less energy. Furthermore, I believe that river fish are not as fit in summer as they are in winter. Because of the heavier flow rates, for want of a better term, the fish are constantly active as they combat winter's stronger currents. So, especially in the summer months, successful river anglers must be very careful in the handling of the fish and must learn to consider their every need.

Basic Code of Practice

Don't keep specimen fish out of the water for longer than is absolutely necessary. After unhooking, which should be done on an unhooking mat, place the fish back in the water in your landing-net while you sort out your weighing equipment. Don't forget to wet your sack and weigh-sling. Weigh the fish as quickly as possible, put it in your sack, and site the sack in deep water with a steady flow in one direction only – that is, not in an eddy. You may need to wade to reach deeper water, and if you get wet in the process, you must not mind. There won't be time to find a suitable sacking site after you have caught your barbel, so do it beforehand. Before leaving the sack to set up your camera or to do any other job, ensure that the fish is facing upstream, that it is upright and that it is breathing satisfactorily. All this can be determined by gently feeling the fish's movements through the sack. Ensure that the sack is

dark coloured, that it is big enough for the fish, and that it has sufficient and adequate water flow. Too many holes for water flow is far preferable to too few. (See also the National Rivers Authority's requirements for retention sacks in Chapter 4.) Each sack must contain only one fish.

Remember to keep checking the situation and the breathing of the fish. When you are certain that the fish is perfectly happy, then, and only then, can you leave it to do whatever it is you have to do, such as set up the camera gear. Keep all this as close as possible to where you have sited the sack. If it is necessary to keep the background unidentifiable, use an umbrella to hide it or have it blanked out in the final picture. Don't carry the fish further than is necessary simply to disguise the venue.

Do everything you can to minimise the time that the fish is out of the water – for example, mark out where the photographs are to be taken and roughly focus the camera (if a tripod is to be used, even critical focusing can be carried out). Ensure that there is sufficient film in the camera (it is unacceptable to keep a fish out of the water while a film is replaced). Do everything you can to minimise the time that the fish is out of the water. You should aim for less than a minute, which is longer than you think. And I know that this period of time is realistic, because I have done all that is necessary in less time than this on many occasions.

Do not carry a fish unless it is in a sack, or, initially, in the landing-net. It is notoriously difficult to carry a fish in bare hands, and if you do drop it, permanent damage could be sustained. I have discussed this topic with people who handle live fish every day of their working lives, and, without exception, all say that fish are liable to be dropped when they are carried by hand, no matter how experienced the person. For the same reason, keep fish as close to the ground as possible when taking pictures, and it won't hurt you to get your knees wet in the process.

Before bringing fish out of the water for weighing and/or photographing, ensure that it is fit enough for the ordeal. Strong body and gill movements are a must. Also, it must be sturdy enough to face upstream and to stay upright of its own volition. If there is any doubt at all, the fish must not be removed from the water. And

● *The condition of Bob Buteux's 6lb 7oz chub is a credit to its previous captors*

if there is any sign that the fish is becoming weaker, rather than stronger, from its stay in the sack, release it and do not remove it again from the water. This may seem a high price to pay, but it is infinitely preferable to go without pictures than to have the death of a big fish on your conscience – a death that, besides all other considerations, will prevent other anglers from experiencing the thrill of catching that particular fish.

I believe that most mistakes regarding the fish's welfare are made at the moment of release. It is perfectly understandable that anglers should want to return the fish to its environment as soon as possible, but it should not be returned until it is strong enough to swim away under its own volition.

If it is removed from the water for photographing, the fish should be carried back to the river in the wet sack. It should be held upright and facing upstream in deep water and the water must have an easy and steady current. If you have to wade to find such an area and get wet in the process, it is not important. When caring for a captured fish, pick some suitable places prior to the event, so saving time and having one less thing to think about. Once back in the water, the fish should be nursed for however long it takes for it to regain its strength. Signs to look for are even gill movements that become stronger and more regular with the passage of time.

Eventually, the fish will let you know when it is ready by swimming out of your hands. However, don't be misled into believing that this is the end of your responsibility. You must still keep an eye on the fish in case it turns belly up. If it does, retrieve the fish with the landing-net and begin the nursing procedure anew. If the preceding guidelines have been observed, this is rarely necessary.

It is now well known that carp are extremely long lived – fifty years is not exceptional. It is less well known that barbel also live to a ripe old age. I have taken photographs of the same individual barbel with more than ten years between captures, and it was an adult fish when the original pictures were taken. Who is to say just how old such fish are? So the message is clear: if you want to catch specimen fish, take the trouble to find out how to look after them properly. There is much more to know than is described in these brief guidelines. Don't be afraid to ask experienced anglers their views, as they will be only too pleased to help and advise you. And if you should see someone not doing the right thing, you must not be afraid to advise them. In the unlikely event that you are verbally abused for your advice, you must not mind – everything is worthwhile in the interest of and the care of a specimen fish.

● *If he were fishing today, it is certain that Jack Hilton wouldn't be using old-fashioned meshes, such as those shown here*

11
Good Days

This chapter will describe some memorable captures of big river fish, with accounts from Roger Newman, Ray Clarke, Bob Buteux and Tony Arbery. A few of my own experiences are included.

The Biggest Chub I Have Ever Seen

For most people, a phone call in the small hours from *Angling Times* would be very annoying. For me, however, it provided a welcome break in the monotonous tedium of yet another eleven hours spent working on the night-shift. Even a phone call from Adrian Curtis was not too much to suffer. Adrian asked me if I would be prepared to go out to the Hampshire Avon to photograph and witness a big chub for *Angling Times*. He explained that the fish was 7lb 10oz. Because it would not have been the first time that a mistake had been made, I asked him if he was sure that it was a big chub and not a small common carp, which are common in the Avon. Adrian assured me that the captor, Roger Newman, was an experienced angler who was well known in match-fishing circles, besides being the owner of a tackle shop. He should know the difference between a carp and a chub. However, he suggested that I should ring him and check for myself.

For a few minutes, I considered the situation: the time was well past midnight and I had to telephone an experienced angler, whom I had never met, and ask him if he knew the difference between a chub and a carp. With some trepidation, I dialled the number.

Roger Newman was obviously awaiting my call, for he answered almost immediately. Within a short time I realised that he knew what he was talking about. Nevertheless, I had to ask him the question I was dreading most: was he absolutely certain that the fish

in question was a chub.

After a long pause, Roger calmly replied that he was completely certain about its identification – it was definitely a chub. And, even though he had caught chub in the past to over 6lb, this one was by far the biggest he had ever seen.

Roger went on to explain that there might be a small discrepancy in the weight. His scales were made by Contessa and designed primarily for match-fishing purposes. This particular model only weighs up to 7lb, and the further 10oz were estimated from the second revolution of the pointer. As the balance was not designed to be used in this way, Roger was unsure how accurate this might prove.

Roger then gave me an account of the capture. The successful method was long-trotting in a swim just 2ft deep. Initially, Roger fed and baited the hook with maggot and caster. However, when he got the chub going, he changed the hook-bait to bread-flake. It has been his experience that chub much bigger than the norm are more prepared to accept flake than maggots and/or casters. The big chub came on his last cast of the day when it was proving difficult, because of the failing light, to see the float. The fight was one of powerful, dogged resistance and Roger realised that he had latched into something special. He kept his cool and played the fish carefully, and eventually it had to go in the waiting net. His tackle included a Drennan Stickfloat rod, a crow quill Avon float and a 2lb bs line tied direct to a size 12 Kamasan hook.

Roger and I made arrangements to meet early the next morning at the venue and, finally, all this information was passed back to Adrian Curtis.

Not long after dawn, my son Tony, who did not want

● *Every scrap of available cover is being used to full advantage by Jack Hilton*

Leicestershire County Council

No. 4553

TRADING STANDARDS DEPARTMENT   Weights & Measures Act 1985

Name ...... L. ARBERY ......

All enquiries to:-

Address ... 179 PARK RD NTH UXBRIDGE MDX,   3 GREY FRIARS

LEICESTER

Account Address if different ......

Date ... 29 - 1 . 90 ......   Issued by ... Harry M Whitehead

LF & LO/INTOX.   **CERTIFICATE OF TEST**

Measuring Instruments

							LF & LO	
Instrument Serial No.							C	Container
Instrument Type							M	Multi
Result of test							S	Single
Reading after test							INTOX.	
Reading before test							A	n/e 5fl. oz.
No. gall/litres/withdrawn							B	Other

Weights	Correct.	Incor.	Adjust.	Stamped	Measures
Over 10lb/5Kg – less than 5gr/500mg					
Other weights					

Weighing Instruments	34lb/15Kg & under			224lb/100Kg & under			560lb/250Kg & under			2240lb/ 1 tonne & under		22400lb/ 10 tonne & under		67200lb/ 30 tonne & under		Over 67200lb/ 30 tonne	
Cost Code	1	2	3	4	5	6	7	8	9	10	11	12	13	14	15	16
Type	Result of Test	Imp or Met	Imp & Met	Elec Pr Comp	Imp or Met	Imp & Met	Elec Pr Comp	Imp or Met	Imp & Met	Imp or Met	Imp & Met	Imp or Met	Imp & Met	Imp or Met	Imp & Met	Imp or Met	Imp & Met

Other equipment/Report or test under Section 74/Remarks

6 olb. SPECIMEN HUNTER SCALE.

FOUND TO BE ACCURATE TO WITHIN ½ oz THROUGHOUT ITS TESTED RANGE (0 TO 14 lb.)

DO NOT USE THIS SPACE

NO CHARGE	✓	RECEIPT NO.		INVOICE NO.		Processed by

IC = Inspected Correct   VS = Verified Stamped   VS(P) = Verified Stamped (Price Change)   VR(P) = Verified Rejected
IR = Inspected Rejected   VR = Verified Rejected   IOR = Incorrect in other respects   (Price Change)

CP.99
Rev. 7/86

● *Roger Newman returns his 7lb 8oz chub, the biggest fully authenticated chub for years*

● Fig 19 *Weights and Measures certificate confirming that the balance used to weigh Roger Newman's 7lb 8oz chub and the author's 14lb barbel, was accurate to within ½oz*

to miss seeing such a remarkable fish, and I were surprised to find that a number of people had already gathered to witness the fish. I thought I knew what to expect a big chub to look like, having seen more than one 6-pounder in my time, but I was wrong. Roger's chub was reposing in one of those giant keep-nets and its size absolutely astonished me – it was colossal! And, despite witnessing carp to over 40lb, and a host of other big fish down the years, it was the most impressive fish that I had ever seen.

After introducing himself, Roger told me that his big chub had already been reweighed at a local shop, where it registered 7lb 4oz. After making it clear that I didn't necessarily dispute this weight, I explained that I needed to weigh the fish personally before I could verify it. My weigh-sling was wetted, wrung out and suspended on my Reuban Heaton Specimen balance, which was then put to zero. In order that the scales would not have to be laid down, perhaps disturbing the setting and hence the accuracy in the process, Tony slipped the chub into the weigh-sling. This in turn was hung on the balance where it registered 7lb 8oz. Afterwards, the weigh-sling was checked and found to be still registering zero.

At this point, within reason, Roger wanted to claim the chub at 7lb 8oz, but I wanted to be absolutely sure that my balance was accurate. I had never had reason to doubt its accuracy before, but the shopkeeper's reading caused me concern.

On returning home, my local Weights and Measures Department proved not at all helpful and *Angling Times*, through Adrian Curtis, received a similar response in their area. So, to see if they could resolve the problem, I telephoned the makers of my balance, Reuban Heaton & Company. To cut a long story short, they could and they would. All I had to do was to travel the 100 miles or so to Market Bosworth with the scales.

The following Monday my balance was checked using certified weights and it proved accurate to within ¹⁄₂₀z; this error was to the good, indicating that Roger's chub, if anything, weighed a little more than 7lb 8oz. Then, by a stroke of good fortune, the local Weights and Measures inspector arrived. I explained the situation and he checked my balance using his own certified weights. The results tallied. The small error of ¹⁄₂₀z remained constant throughout the tested range, right up to 14lb. It was fortuitous that the balance was checked at this weight, because shortly after it was used to weigh another outstanding fish – my own 14lb barbel, a fish that was to earn for me the most coveted

and prestigious award in big fish angling, the Drennan Cup.

It is my belief that at the time of capture, Roger Newman's large chub probably weighed 7lb 10oz, his original weighing. A weight loss of some 2oz overnight, in a fish of this size, is entirely consistent with past experiences. It was a pity that we could not have verified the weight earlier. This incident clearly demonstrates that if you are fortunate enough to catch an outsize specimen, you should get it accurately weighed and witnessed as soon as possible. You don't want to let the chance of a record or any other major prize slip through your fingers.

The front page of *Angling Times*, 31 January 1990, carried Adrian Curtis' report, under the headline: 'Biggest Chub for Years'.

Best for years! Chippenham Cruisers match ace Roger Newman is all smiles as he cradles Britain's biggest fully-authenticated chub for years.

As we reported last week, this stunning 7lb 8oz beauty – just two ounces short of the British record – fell to trotted breadflake from a swim on the Hampshire Avon at Fordingbridge.

The capture crowned a super year for Roger, who runs the Fish 'n' Shoot tackle shop in Bath, Avon, and earns a Drennan Cup weekly award.

(NB   Since then, G. F. Smith's 1913 Royalty caught chub of 8lb 4oz has been reinstated as the current British record for the species.)

The Record Roach Story
by Ray Clarke

My friend Fred Beech invited me to join him for a weekend's fishing trip on his club's stretch of the Dorset Stour. This would be the first time that either of us had fished that famous river.

Fred and I arrived at the venue on the afternoon of Friday 26 October 1990, after a wet and windy, yet uneventful journey. The bailiff was waiting, as Fred had asked him to show us around the fishery. My initial impression was that the river, though still low from the effects of the past hot summer, looked tempting, having areas of steady flow and a nice tinge of colour.

Although I had not planned to fish until the following morning, I had already picked my swim. This spot looked very inviting – fastish water running into a deepish pool, where the water gently eddied, before a nice run-out. There was a willow tree to the left of the swim and a deep hole to my right.

We reached the gate to the fishery at 8am the following morning, just as the farmer was about to lock it. To save us the ¾-mile walk down to the river, I offered him a fiver to take us on his tractor. He refused the money but gave us permission to drive down in our van. As we drove off, I threw him the fiver anyway. It was still raining and, if anything, the wind was even stronger than the previous day. The river was carrying more colour and running faster, too – facts that did nothing to improve my optimism.

Because I didn't want to disturb any fish present, I tackled up my three outfits in the meadow well away from the river: 1) 13ft Daiwa rod; stick-float, carrying 8 No 4 shot; 3lb main-line; 1.7lb bottom. 2) 13ft Ashurst rod; waggler float, carrying 4 BBs; 2lb main-line; 1lb bottom. 3) 11ft John Wilson quiver-tip rod; block-end feeder; 2.5lb main-line tied direct to the hook.

Roach were my main target and I was really looking for one over 2lb because I had caught many just under that magic figure, but none over. This stretch of the Stour has the pedigree to produce roach well over 2lb, in addition to big specimens of other species. I realised, of course, that my tackle choice would leave me well undergunned if anything like a hard-fighting barbel was hooked.

By the time that I was ready to fish, the rain had increased and the strong upstream wind was blowing straight into my face. Because of these conditions I had chosen the waggler and began to feed casters and hemp into the stream and the deep hole. To my surprise, the swim was not as deep as I had imagined – around 3ft in the stream and 6ft in the hole. The dark colour of the weed fooled me.

By 10.30am I had not had a bite, but some good fish 'topping' further down the pool made me think that the feed was ending up further downstream than I had planned. Long-trotting from my position was not possible because of an intervening weed-bed, so I moved 18yd downstream, taking just the stick-float rod and the bare essentials with me.

Here, the bank was steep, but I got down successfully, although I had to feed and cast upstream. The float ran close to the bank and toward me, then down-stream ending in an eddy close to a fallen tree. There was a little flow here and the float could be held back, the bait searching right in among the submerged branches.

By 11.15am, still without a bite, despite scaling down to a single caster mounted on a size 18 hook, I was almost ready to give up. But although I was wet and cold, I knew that it was worth it, so I gritted my teeth and carried on.

My next cast produced a bite and at last a fish was on – but not for long. It took off powerfully downstream and, despite my backwinding furiously, he smashed the hook-link. I could not say what it was, but it was a good fish – a chub, barbel, carp or a good eel. This lost fish encouraged me to step up the tackle and fish a 3lb line tied direct to a size 16 barbless Kamasan B510. (This is not only one of the best hooks around, but is a major factor in fishes' welfare – torn lips are a thing of the past when extracting these hooks.)

At 11.35am another fish was hooked. Like the previous one, it headed downstream toward the dead tree, but with the increased power at my disposal, the tables were turned and it was prevented from reaching the danger. But the fish fought for some minutes before it was safely in the landing-net. A chub in great condition weighing 4lb 5oz, it was the hardest fighting chub that I had ever caught.

No further bites were forthcoming in the following 45 minutes, so another move was decided upon. The next piece of water I fancied was at the bottom of a very steep, high bank. Conditions made fishing from the top impossible and waterlogged reeds at the bottom suggested that they covered water too deep for me to stand in, although I was wearing thigh-waders. As I was about to move on, I noticed a cow-pat on the reeds. I thought that if those reeds were strong enough to support a cow, they were strong enough to support me.

By now the rain had stopped and a watery sun illuminated the scene, although the wind was as strong as ever. Fifteen minutes passed before the first fish was hooked in the new cow-pat swim. It dived into the reeds on which I was standing and broke my line adjacent to a shot. Perhaps the line was damaged because I had squeezed on the shot too tightly.

After retackling with an identical set-up, I took a break to give the swim chance to settle back down. It was 1.30pm before I was fishing the cow-pat swim once more. Some hemp and a few casters were thrown in upstream, followed by my float. On the very first cast

● *Ray Clarke's record roach is measured. From the nose to the fork of its tail it was 17½in (*Terry Lampard)

as the float came under my rod-top, about 10ft out, it disappeared and another good fish was hooked. Like the previous fish, it dived into the reeds under my feet but, this time, pressure from my end brought it back out. It darted into the faster water at the narrowest part of the swim and, from its dark back, appeared to be a bream. Then a flash of silver and red revealed a different story – it was a roach, and a big one at that.

With the fish safely in the net and myself well back in the field, I realised that this was not only a big roach, it was an enormous specimen. Not only had I caught my first 2-pounder, but my first 3-pounder as well. Taking the roach in the landing-net back to my tackle to weigh it, I met Fred who was amazed at the size of my catch.

The reading on the scales revealed that here was more than just an enormous roach; this was no less than a new British record! Immediately Fred set off to find another angler who we had seen fishing earlier, to act as

a witness. The roach was kept in my keep-net while I awaited Fred's return, which seemed interminable. I chain-smoked trying to keep calm; I was almost scared to have caught such a momentous fish. To keep my mind occupied I thought of my brothers; Dave, who sadly died on a fishing trip and Melvyn, who continued to teach and take me fishing before emigrating to Australia.

Fred had obviously missed the other angler, because I noticed him get up from the bank, between me and where Fred had disappeared. To attract the lad's attention, I shouted, waved and whistled, and finally he noticed me. I set off toward him carrying the fish, keep-net and all. My luck was certainly in that day because it turned out to be none other than Terry Lampard, one of the most successful anglers in England who is well known and respected by everybody in the big-fish world. Terry could not believe the size of the roach and

● *Ray Clarke proudly poses with his 4lb 3oz current record roach, caught from the Dorset Stour, on 27 October 1990 (*Terry Lampard)

we put it back in the water, still in the keep-net, while Terry set up his camera and weighing gear. On both Terry's and my scales the fish weighed 4lb 2oz, but when subsequently checked, both read 1oz light – so my big roach actually weighed 4lb 3oz.

Photographs were taken of the roach before it was returned to the river. I realised that this act might jeopardise my claim for official recognition of the roach by the British Record Fish Committee, but none of us present wanted to put this magnificent creature through any further distress by keeping it longer than necessary. And, even though I knew that it would be worth a great deal of money displayed in a glass-case, I had no desire to kill it. I just hope that it continues to thrive and one day gives another angler the thrill that I experienced – that of landing a record roach.

A Winter Bonus

The rains had at last arrived. From Ringwood down to Christchurch the Avon Valley was, for a while, almost one vast lake. It was a paradise for wading birds and a perfect sanctuary for the seabirds that flocked to the area to escape the harsh conditions of the coasts in winter. Now the Avon was back to just within its banks, but only the previous week the rising waters had threatened the very heart of Christchurch.

I made my way alone, over the soft, slippery turf of the fields bordering the river. It was hardly believable that here I was on the banks of the famous Royalty on a pleasant day in winter, with nobody else in sight. Of course, the never-ending procession of cars continued to buzz over the bypass bridge, and yet here was I, in splendid isolation, less than a mile from the bustling centre of Christchurch. It felt unreal.

My feet slipped and slithered even more as I neared the river's edge, the sweet scent of the water-mint deliciously heady in the crisp, bright air. It was gin-clear. This condition of the water was noted with more than a hint of satisfaction. Chub would be my aim, at least until lunchtime.

The swim I had in mind was some way downstream, near the bypass bridge (how fish like bridges). Here a small stream enters the main river. This stream, which is dry in summer, was today swiftly carrying water drawn from immediately above the Railway Bridge pool (this pool is probably the most consistent barbel-

producing area on the Royalty); it re-enters the river here just upstream of the bypass bridge on the east bank).

Under conditions when the Avon carries much less water than it was that day, the silt arrested here over the years formed an island. The only evidence of this I could see in the form of a stem or two of sedge which had somehow resisted the floods of the previous weeks and which were standing bent yet unbroken, their upper limbs bedecked with debris from less durable plants, stranded here by the receding water. Also stranded, among the flotsam back in the field, a fish's carcass caught my attention. A once beautiful fish, the noble salmon now lay rotting, mutilated almost beyond recognition by the riverside scavengers. I felt sad for the salmon, yet was it not true that even in death it was still fulfilling a purpose – that of providing food for Mother Nature's less loved, yet no less important other children? I walked on in contemplative mood.

The chosen pitch arrived at, my trusty Avon rod was assembled well away from the river. A 6lb line, a link-leger and a size 6 hook completed the simple rig. (This was long before those two delightful weapons, the Drennan Light Feeder and Bomb rods were invented.) From this position, the swim was surveyed. The aforementioned stream entered the river to my immediate right. To the left no features of any consequence were visible for about 30 yd or so, but here was situated the 'dead-cut', immediately upstream of the bypass bridge. This dead-cut was once part of the river proper. Here, however, the river made a 180° turn, and at about the time the bypass was built, the river's course was straightened, as is the policy of today's water authority engineers. Now only the dead-cut remains, as a mute testament to how the river once used to be. Big pike have been taken from the dead-cut, and often in winter the pike anglers are present in numbers. On that particular day however, there was not another living soul in sight.

My seat, landing-net and creel were positioned with slow, deliberate care. I try to implement Dick Walker's advice, 'study to be quiet', at all times, but particularly so when the chub are the quarry. Flake from a freshly bought loaf was my only bait. Bob Buteux taught me

---

● *The author's heaviest chub to date – a 6lb 9oz specimen from the Dorset Stour, caught in February 1992*

the value and use of bread-flake. Nobody that I know of has more experience or had more success with flake than Bob. (Which is hardly surprising – 'cos he won't use anything else!) As soon as the tackle settled, the rod-tip rattled. Instantly, and instinctively, I pushed the rod toward the fish, giving it some slack line. The fish took up all the slack line and pulled the rod-tip around a further 9in or so. The answering strike connected and

---

● (inset) *Tony Arbery's heaviest chub to date – a 6lb 4oz Dorset Stour specimen*

● *Hugh Miles with a brace of 2lb roach from the Longford Estate stretch on the Hampshire Avon (Bob James)*

● *Almost too much of a good thing! Peter Stone fishes a flooded River Thames (Peter Stone)*

---

a chub was soon in the landing-net. This was only a 'taster', weighing about 2½lb.

An hour or so later, a repeat performance was enacted, and a much better chub pulled the balance down to 4lb 14oz. This fish fought extremely well, taking full advantage of the heavy water, and some four or five minutes elapsed before it could be netted. A prolonged battle was something I could have done without, for past experience in this swim had shown that other chub in the shoal would not tolerate such disturbances. They would now show even more caution, and, bearing in mind their normal infamous wariness, I knew that they

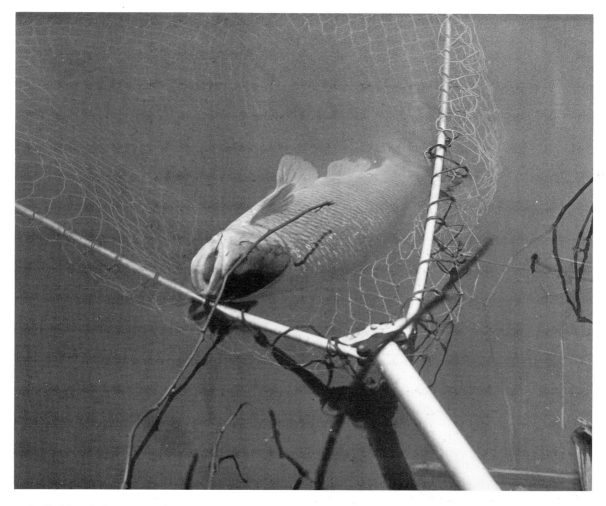

● *A 4lb 14oz chub comes to the net*

would be almost impossible to catch. Today was no exception.

The swim was rested for a full hour before I recast, but the chub still would not bite properly. Digs and leans on the rod-top betrayed chub remaining in the swim. Despite striking as quick as my reactions allowed, the chub were quicker still. A change of tactics was needed.

Another tactic learned from Bob Buteux came to mind which requires (for right-handers) that the rod is held in the right hand, while the left hand holds the line, keeping a few feet of slack available. At the first indication of a bite, the line is released by the left hand. You then quickly count to three and strike. It sometimes

works. The idea behind the scheme is to fool the chub into believing that it has freed the bait from the tackle, allaying its suspicions. The count to three gives it time to get the bait back in its mouth, but not enough time to feel the resistance of the tackle once more. It works sometimes and that is often enough to make it a worthwhile pursuit.

The following two strikes missed, but the third strike met with living resistance. I knew at once that it was chub, but it didn't take much longer to realise from the fight that it wasn't hooked in the mouth.

Knowing that the chub was foul-hooked did not make me any less keen to land it, even though it would not count, for it felt like a good one. I wanted to see just how good it was. Then everything went solid and I swore to myself for letting the fish weed me. Try as I might, the tackle could not be freed and reluctantly I pulled for a break. The weed-bed to which my tackle was firmly attached obviously did not like this treatment, and to my utter amazement pulled back savagely.

Now weed-beds are not renowned for behaviour of this kind, and while I struggled to regain control of the situation, I began to realise that I was in contact with an underwater adversary of extreme power. And what power it possessed can be gauged by the fact that its first head-long rush took it upstream, past the submerged island. This, of course, was in direct opposition to the Hampshire Avon in full spate.

I conjectured that it was a salmon and concluded that I had pulled out of the chub and foul-hooked a salmon. I determined to try to land it, just to see how big it was. Other, more dedicated chub anglers may have decided to pull for a break, for this battle was sure to 'kill' the swim for days. However, I enjoy a fighting fish and whether it sports an extra fin or not is of no consequence to me.

Its initial rush stopped, the fish sulked on the bottom in midstream. To let it rest, would, I considered, be courting disaster, for the battle was one-sided enough now, without letting the fish regain its strength at every opportunity. In this situation, my tackle would be under-strength at the height of the summer. Now, in winter, with a raging torrent to contend with, it was hopelessly inadequate.

I pointed the rod down the line toward the fish and hand-lined as fiercely as the 6lb line permitted. An effect was immediately forthcoming and stunning in its violence. My adversary swam downstream as fast as its fins would carry it in the fast current, with me following in its wake as best as I could. With my rod in one hand and my landing-net (optimistically, I admit) tucked under my free arm, I stumbled on after the fish, albeit a good distance in arrear.

As I approached the bridge, I realised that if the fish went through, all would be lost. Fortunately, it took a sharp left-hand turn and went into the dead-cut. It did not stay there for long, however, for, under the full pressure my 6lb line could muster, the fish effortlessly made 20yd up the cut in approximately an equal number of seconds. Without a pause, it did an about-turn and rifled back into the main river. As it did so, I caught the first glimpse of my adversary; it was not a salmon but a green/grey shadow – that could only mean a pike! It was a good one, too, maybe as heavy as 16–18lb.

Upstream she went again, but she seemed to be tiring, as she failed to reach the island. She turned into the slack in the lee of the island, where I had been chub fishing serenely a short while ago. It paused here for a second or two, then shot downstream again like a rocket.

I felt pangs of panic, for surely the pike realised that its sanctuary lay open, so long as it continued downstream below the bridge, for my tackle could not bring a fish of this size back upstream against the push of the raging torrent. My luck held, however, and once again the pike turned sharply into the dead-cut. This was its final undoing, for I had learned well the lessons of our last encounter here. I resolved at this point that she would not make the river again – and she didn't.

I let her swim right into the cut, as far as was practicable, under very little pressure from me. When I took up the challenge once more, it was now with a limited measure of confidence; the tables had been turned and now I called the tune. From this position, the pike would have to fight all the way back to the river. In fact, she never made it, but she got very close.

The netting took place just inside the junction of the cut and the river. As I lifted my prize on to the bank, I was surprised to see the pike's massive bulk and to hear a loud cheer. I looked up to see that the traffic had stopped and there was a crowd of spectators on the bypass bridge. If I had known either of these facts a few minutes earlier, my nerve probably would have failed me, and this tale may have had a very different ending. Tenderly, I carefully weighed her, then called to the gallery, 'Pike – 25lb 1oz!' Slowly, the knot of people dispersed and the traffic once more began its continuous cacophony.

A walk up to the 'house-pool' found a fellow who was obliging enough to take some pictures for me. Unfortunately, the sprocket holes tore in my film and the film was ruined. Hence, I have no photographic record of the fish that gave me one of the most memorable battles of my fishing career.

Incidentally, this pike was hooked in the mouth (scissors), although it took some time to convince Bill Quinlan of the fact. Whether the chub that was originally hooked went down, or out of its mouth, I have, of course, no way of knowing.

A remarkable coincidence is that both the late Bill Warren and Bob Buteux have caught pike in similar circumstances and the three pike weighed within ounces of each other. Mine, as already stated, was 25lb 1oz, Bill's is reputed to have weighed 25lb 8oz, and Bob's, at 25lb 12oz, was the heaviest of the trio.

● *Caught in similar circumstances to my 25lb 1oz pike, Bill Warren's 25lb 8oz fish . . .*

A Dream Come True

The preparations for the 1989–90 winter's fishing began long before the winter. Many trips were made to assess likely venues and even to weigh up particular swims. There are good reasons for reconnaissance visits and, even accounting for the price of petrol, etc, it is time and money well spent. I am not discounting the obvious consideration that, if left until the fishing trip proper, time spent on reconnaissance will be at the expense of time actually spent fishing. But let us discuss some further valid reasons for preparatory visits prior to actually fishing.

To assess the nature of the bottom of the river in a fancied area, you can not beat actually seeing it. In

winter, the river's level is usually much higher than in summer and therefore there are precious few opportunities to see its bed at this time. Conversely, when the water is low and clear not only can you see the features and constituents that make up the river-bed, you may also see the fish as well. No matter how well intentioned, or how knowledgeable, your informants, there is no more certain way of knowing that the fish of the size and/or species you seek exist than by seeing them with your own eyes.

In warmer weather there are more anglers on the bank. Most, being either locals or regulars to the stretch, know much about their own waters. Talking to these people can be very rewarding; it seems that there is much less secrecy among river fishermen than among other anglers. Also, with more time at your disposal,

● *. . . and Bob Buteux's 25lb 12oz Stour monster* (Bob Buteux)

because you are not hurrying to get fishing, you will find talking to people other than anglers can be beneficial, too. For example, keen gardeners spend lots of time in their gardens and on more than one occasion I have learned of the capture of a big fish by talking to the person whose property borders the river. There is also much to be gained by meeting landowners, farmers, and the like; if you are courteous, polite and present-able, you may even be given special dispensation to fish at times other than those considered normal. So long as you plainly demonstrate that you are not going to poach the landowner's salmon or wildfowl, and you know how to behave while you are on private estates, you may succeed in talking yourself into some exclusive fishing. Never underestimate the value of local information, and remember this maxim: if you find a fool in the countryside, you no doubt took one along with you!

Actual fishing time may also be saved by learning all the access routes; there is nothing more frustrating, after a long and tiring walk to a fancied swim, to see someone beat you to it because they know a short-cut. Be careful to park your car where it will cause no nuisance or annoyance. The loads transported by tractors and their trailers, etc are sometimes wider than normal. You certainly won't make a farmer's day by blocking his access, and it won't do much to improve your demeanour if, on returning to your car, you discover it minus a front wing or even worse.

If, like many other successful anglers, you take the trouble to pre-bait sensibly, you will undoubtedly reap rich rewards. Of course, this aspect of successful fishing has always been understood, so why do so many anglers continue to ignore this important facet? Down through the centuries, notable angling writers, including Izaac Walton, J. W. Martin and Richard Walker, have pointed out that if fish eat many items of a particular food without ill-effects, it will obviously take them longer to associate that food with danger. Consequently, more fish are caught before that bait 'blows'. So it is a mystery why so many anglers ignore the value and importance of pre-baiting.

As so often happens, the Christmas holidays coincided with the first of the season's earnest fishing trips to the rivers. There had been some rain just prior to Christmas. However, by the time my friends and I arrived in Dorset, the waters had receded and the rain was just a memory. Notwithstanding that fact, the Stour was still much higher than its summer level, yet the water was clear and bright, and its temperature was 44°F. All this meant just one thing to our little group – chub.

There were too many of us to fish together, so some went to Throop, and Bob Harrington, Bob Buteux and I fished further upstream. As it was a pleasant winter's day during the Christmas holidays, there were plenty of people on the banks. The one thing we learned from these anglers was that, although the conditions looked ideal, the fishing was proving far from easy. And when, at last, we found some unoccupied, decent-looking water, it did not take long for us to discover that they were right. Nevertheless, we persevered and ended the day with just five chub between us – but, each one was a 4-pounder. This sometimes is a feature of winter river fishing: on certain days the few fish that are prepared to feed are all very much the same size. On that particular day, link-legered bread-flake proved the successful method. On returning to our holiday cottage that evening, the remainder of the party had a similar tale to tell – few fish had been caught but they were of a high average size.

For the remaining few days of our holiday, I fished on my own and blanked. However, this did not deter my aim for that winter – to catch a personal best barbel. The others ribbed me unmercifully each evening, especially as they had caught some very respectable specimens; in fact, Bob Buteux had improved his personal best river-caught roach to 2lb 9oz. I was not bothered by their leg-pulling, as it was all good natured. Besides, I had done my homework well and I was happy to fish the rest of the winter without a bite, for I was very confident that I was doing the right thing, in the right place, at the right time.

The following weekend I was back, this time accompanied by my son, Tony. Again, the Stour looked perfect for chub, with the added bonus that the temperature had climbed to 46°F. The main part of the day was spent pursuing chub, with late afternoons and evenings reserved for further attempts to get a very big barbel. The chub fishing proved very successful: the two days produced ten fish all over 3lb, the best being 5lb 1oz, my first 5-pounder of the winter. The barbel again proved elusive, however, I had my first barbel bite of the season, but missed it. Tony's results for the weekend were roughly similar, apart from one important difference: he 'nailed' his only barbel bite and it weighed 9lb 14oz. All the chub were caught on flake; both barbel bites came to meat. As normal, we touch-legered, feeling the line for bites.

● *After a hard day out on the bank, Bob Buteux and Bob Harrington relax in our Christmas holiday cottage (*Bob Buteux)

I travelled down on my own the next weekend. Apart from the water level being lower, conditions were similar. The whole time was spent barbel fishing, but again no barbel bites were forthcoming. Two, not unwelcome, chub picked up the meat; they weighed 3lb 1oz and 4lb 4oz.

Earlier in this chapter I told the story of Roger Newman's monster 7lb 8oz chub, events which occurred on the following Thursday. After leaving Roger and phoning these events into Adrian Curtis at the *Angling Times*, Tony and I had breakfast, then went to Throop. The water was clear and 44°F, and the chub were going absolutely crazy. We soon lost count of how many we had caught and, even though none was anything special, we weren't complaining. Next day we anticipated a great slaughter, but some subtle change had taken place and we struggled to get a bite. So, by late afternoon, we decided a change of venue was required – a very good move, as it turned out.

As dusk approached, I found some barbel that were prepared to give small bites. After missing a few, Tony came along and I invited him to sit down and try his luck alongside me. On his first cast Tony experienced

the ultimate thrill in river fishing – a good, strong barbel bite.

Tony whispered hoarsely through clenched teeth, 'I think it's a little one, Dad.' From the steady bend in Tony's rod I thought that it was anything but little, but kept my peace. I didn't want to make Tony unnecessarily nervous. There was nothing spectacular about the fight at all, but on lifting the net I knew, without any shadow of doubt, that here was a new personal best for my son. And so it proved; at 11lb 14oz, it was also a family best and, with dimensions of length (from nose to fork of tail) 29 ¾in, girth 19¾in, it was one of the best conditioned barbel that I have ever had the privilege of witnessing.

Then came the big storms. They did not prevent me from travelling to Dorset, but they did sometimes prevent me from fishing. On one trip, although the river was over its banks and in the fields, I tried to get on to the banks of the Avon. A masterful plan was worked out. After gaining access to a field that gradually sloped down to the river, I would wade to the edge of the river and stand up to fish. All was going to plan. There was I, rod made up and ready to go in one hand, my landing-net in the other, making steady but deliberate progress in ever-deepening water, towards the river. The water was lapping near the top of my waders, but there wasn't much further to go, for I could plainly see the rise in the ground, adjacent to the actual riverbank, where it would be child's play to fish from. What I couldn't see and, I suppose, in the excitement of the moment had forgotten, was the ditch. This feature is insignificant under normal conditions, but it was a catastrophic trap for the unwary. For me, one moment everything seemed to be under control, then suddenly I was under filthy, freezing water.

Immediately, my waders filled up and my woolly hat, now waterlogged and increased in weight several-fold, slipped over my eyes. A more efficient blindfold would be difficult to envisage. I could not remove the offending garment because the hood of my waterproof suit was keeping it firmly in place, and my hands were full anyway. I don't know how I came out of that predicament unscathed, and the faces on the passers-by as I squelched back to my car had a look of amazement.

At all times, a complete set of dry clothing is kept in my car for just such an emergency and it was but the work of a few minutes to regain my composure. Undeterred, however, I then went to a stretch of the Avon with higher banks and fished for a few hours with no success.

Next day the Kennet was fished for barbel. Although the water was high and coloured, it was two chub, both 4-pounders, that fell for the lobworm offering.

At every opportunity the ritual journey was made to Dorset. On at least one occasion I did not even stop there; I just turned the car round and came back home. Those storms cost me dearly, especially in lost fishing time.

The next time any serious fishing could be practised was the third week in February, when Tony and Keith Griffin were my companions. The water at Throop was almost bank high, clear and 46°F. We could not get started soon enough. Keith began long-trotting a favourite chub swim and was soon amassing an enviable bag of chub. Tony and I wandered off downstream, fishing every likely spot that took our fancy. We reached an area of good-looking water, which is difficult to fish

effectively because of a copse of small trees and bushes growing at the water's edge. Tony took the upper part and I fished from below the copse.

My first cast, using flake for bait, brought a big pull (despite an upstream cast), which resulted in an 8lb 8oz barbel. No sooner had this fish been returned, when Tony struck into another. Instantly, his almost new carbon rod disintegrated with a resounding crack. Miraculously, the line didn't break and the fish was still attached. It was obvious to me that Tony needed help, so I started to get up from my stool to go to his assistance. The next thing that happened was that I fell in the river. Whether I momentarily blacked out or just slipped will never be known. But the fact was that all my gear was in the river, too. Although I could not touch the bottom, it was easy to grasp a tuft of grass on the bank. I called to Tony to come and help me, and Keith also helped to get me back on the bank. Because we were fishing together, the danger was minimal, but if I had been alone, the situation could have been much more serious.

Once more I squelched back to the car to get changed. As Bob Buteux tirelessly (and tiresomely!) keeps reminding me, I must be much more deliberate and careful now I'm not so steady on my 'pins'! He can talk! He's more than ten years older than me; and Bob, you can't fall in the water if you don't go fishing.

Considerably warmer and certainly drier, I recommenced fishing a swim that produces more than its fair share of 'cagey' bites. The fish were at home and, after scaling down to a 2lb line and a size 12 Carbon Specimen hook, a minute piece of crust produced a bite that pulled the quiver-tip around several inches. The hooked fish put up minimal resistance and proved to be a pristine roach of 2lb 1oz. The next bite was even bigger and the hooked fish set off for Christchurch harbour as if its tail was alight! Eventually, a 4lb 6oz chub had to go in the waiting net, but this performance had effectively killed the swim.

This gave me reason enough to change venues (again in my quest for a giant barbel), although Tony and Keith elected to stay. Perhaps the wiser choice was not mine for, while I went biteless, Tony went on to take a very creditable catch which included a 9lb 4oz barbel and a 5lb 8oz chub.

The three of us were all out chubbing very early the

● *A 2lb 4oz Kennet roach for the author*

next day. It was one of those rare occasions in winter – a sunny and bright morning without a hint of overnight frost. Coupled with the rising water temperature, we were very confident, but it was not that easy. By lunchtime, we had not caught a decent fish between us, but between 1 and 3pm the chub fed well. Keith and I both included 4-pounders in our bag; however, Tony topped us again with a cracker weighing 5lb 9oz.

It was even harder the next day. By late afternoon, without a fish between us, Tony and I were ready to leave for home. Keith, however, asked to stay a little longer as, by this time, he was getting a few small bites. While we were waiting for Keith, Tony and I sat side-by-side fishing a swim which, although it looked promising for chub, had never before produced a single bite. This time, though, as soon as my bread-flake hit the bottom, it was taken with the proverbial bang, but the answering strike unaccountably failed to connect. There was no mistake on the next cast, yet the feeble resistance gave no indication that anything special had been hooked. My first inkling of a big chub came as Tony lifted the landing-net around it. Very careful weighing showed that my chub weighed exactly 6lb, my second heaviest at that time.

The final day of the trip again proved difficult, with just a handful of small chub caught, although I did catch a nice roach weighing 1lb 15oz. It was also a similar story the following weekend; my take consisted of just two chub worth weighing – 3lb 14oz and 4lb 8oz. Tony and Keith, however, each caught a double-figure barbel. Keith's weighed 10lb 1oz, Tony's just 1oz more.

In the early hours of Wednesday 7 March, while at work, I began to feel uneasy. Eventually I realised that my instincts were telling me that I ought to be fishing. A couple of days' holiday were hastily arranged before I hurried home for a little sleep. By 10am that morning my estate car once more headed south-westward, Dorset-bound.

After breakfasting, I arrived on the banks at 1pm to find the venue deserted. Taking advantage of this situation, several swims were pre-baited before fishing commenced at the upstream boundary. No bites materialised until the bend swim, where I missed a definite barbel bite by, I suspect, not striking quickly enough. Not long after, two friends arrived, first Richard Graham, then Ron Chant. After chatting for a while, during which the missed bite was mentioned, Richard left and Ron started to fish about 400yd downstream of my position. My swim was first pre-baited with two drop-pers of hemp and one of diced meat, then a flask of tea was shared with Ron, giving my swim a chance to settle down. It was almost thirty minutes before I returned to where I was fishing.

I can do no better here than to refer to my diary:

Fifteen minutes after recasting came a savage barbel pull. Hit it okay and immediately knew it was something special, so yelled for Ron. Silently Ron materialised at my side, crouched down and rolled a cigarette. Then he picked up the landing-net in readiness, but didn't put it in the water. The last thing he wanted to do was snag my line with the net; at least, not if he didn't want an early bath! The hooked barbel fought resolutely with incredible power. There were no savage jerks on the tackle, so reminiscent when playing lesser barbel. (In fact, Ron remarked later, 'The only jerk on the tackle during the whole fight was the one holding the rod!')

Ron flicked away his cigarette end and still the barbel persisted, but my tackle was sound and she was inevitably tiring, but there was still a long way to go. Close to the opposite bank, still deep in the water, the barbel begrudgingly came upstream. Once she was well past me I increased the pressure. Now she had to fight the power of the river's current in addition to the tackle, and this finally broke her resolve. Ron now dipped the landing-net deep in the water. In she went first time; it was 25 minutes since I'd called to Ron. I put my rod down and went to Ron's assistance as he struggled to lift the fish.

And what a fish! Both of us had seen and caught many barbel, including double-figure fish in the past, but we'd never seen anything remotely as big as this one. I suggested a 'record', but being naturally more cautious, Ron estimated 13–13½lb. Ron read the balance . . . a whisker over 14lb! Just 6oz short of Aylmer Tryon's record barbel. The heaviest-ever barbel caught in winter! Joint 4th biggest of modern times! And a different fish to any of the other 14-pounders caught in recent years! Dimensions: 31½in from nose to fork of tail; 18in girth.

I was so excited and thrilled by this event that fishing was abandoned while I phoned the news through to

● *The author's magnificent winter-caught 14lb barbel*

friends such as Bill Quinlan, Bob Buteux, Kevin Clifford and Tony. Their reactions could alone fill a chapter, but I would like to keep those precious memories to myself.

My big barbel picked up meat fished on a size 6 Drennan Carbon Specimen hook. This was presented on a 2in link-leger set-up consisting of ⅜oz bomb stopped 8in from the hook and tied to a 6lb Drennan Specimen Plus line. The reel was a little 2500 Shimano Bait-runner mounted on a Drennan Light Feeder quiver-tip rod. Bites were detected by touch legering – that is, feeling the line for bites. This was my only barbel in thirty-three visits to that stretch. There certainly is no truer fishing maxim than that you must sacrifice quantity for quality.

Together, the 6lb chub and the 14lb barbel earned for me, in my view, the most prestigious award in big-fish angling – the Drennan Cup. To be voted, by my contemporaries, the winner of this award, following the likes of Greg Buxton, Alan Wilson and Martin Hooper, filled me with pride and, undoubtedly, was a dream come true.

The Long Road to My First 6lb Chub
by Bob Buteux

The task of catching big fish deliberately, and with any degree of consistency, demands much thought, effort and downright hard work. Furthermore, I believe that it is better to build up to this stage – to come through the ranks, as it were. If you join a club and go out on their outings, you will learn much about tackle and methods to suit various venues. Undoubtedly, you will catch plenty of small fish at first and, occasionally, 'bump' into bigger specimens, which you will have trouble dealing with on the fine tackle you will probably be using.

● *The author receives, from Peter Drennan himself, the most prestigious and coveted award in big-fish angling, the Drennan Cup*

A memorable example of this scenario happened to me many years ago. During a club match on a flooded River Thames at Sunbury, I hooked a powerful fish which was almost certainly a barbel. Off he went out into the stream and my 1lb hook-link didn't last long. Afterwards, I was shaking so much that it was difficult to tackle up again.

Until this event I was content to catch a 'goer' – that is, a fish over Thames-size limits. (In those days, only fish over a certain size could be weighed-in in Thames matches.) But that lost fish fired an ambition within me. I now yearned to catch fish of a stamp like the one which had smashed my frail match-type tackle so contemptuously – an ambition that continues to burn undiminished even now, so many years later.

The following weekend I was back in the same swim at Sunbury, but my tackle was more substantial this time. I had four bites that second day and all four were barbel. They were not very big by specimen-hunting standards – the best being a 4-pounder – but to me at that time they were absolute whackers. From that moment on, I spent less time on club outings as catching small fish after this incident disinterested me – from now on it was big fish or bust.

I teamed up with a pal, Bert Dell, and our fishing transport in those days was far from ideal. It consisted of two motorcycles, both past their prime. Bert's machine was a 250cc Panther, 1935 vintage, which seized up every 20 miles or so. My own steed was a 1949, 125cc BSA Bantam. On at least one day each weekend during the season, the pair of us would set off, usually before dawn, to one venue or another, the bikes loaded down far more than the designers intended.

Learning was also a slow business as there were very few big fish anglers in those days to help us. We relied mainly upon learning from our own mistakes, and, being as keen as mustard, we felt good in doing what we wanted to do – angling for fish bigger than the norm. There was, however, one big fish angler who we all learned from – Dick Walker. Dick's weekly column in the *Angling Times* answered many questions before we had even asked them. Further queries were answered personally, and in great detail, in a protracted exchange of correspondence between myself and the Master. But not only did Dick answer queries, he also inspired me to keep fishing and not become disillusioned too readily. Yes, I can honestly report that Dick Walker was my own, and countless others', inspiration.

By this time Bert and I kept angling diaries. We took note of air and water temperatures, the colour and level of the water, wind direction, besides recording our successes – and failures. In fact, we noted anything which might, or might not, have a bearing on catching big fish.

Bert and I adapted every new idea to suit our own particular problems. These, in turn, spawned new thinking on many aspects of angling, and our hard-won successes bred in us a new-found confidence. Confidence in angling, as with most other things, is a vital ingredient to eventual success, for if you are confident that you are doing the right thing, in the right place, at the right time, you won't be swayed easily from the path to your goal, and then, eventually, you can't help but succeed.

During that golden era, on August Bank Holiday weekend, 1956, Bert and I decided to make our first-ever pilgrimage to that Mecca for big fish anglers, the Hampshire Avon's Royalty Fishery, at Christchurch, a renowned venue even in those days. With our bikes loaded down even more than usual (we carried camping gear, food, etc, in addition to our tackle), the journey seemed to take for ever. (The roads were not as good then as they are today and there were no motorways.) During that horrendous journey, thoughts of Royalty monsters in the offing, such as 5lb chub and 10lb barbel, kept us going and made me tremble with excited anticipation.

We walked the banks for a while, until at last we saw some big fish among the lush weed. In those days, at that time of year, the water was gin-clear and you could see most of the bottom, except in the occasional deep pool or in the runs between prolific beds of lush streamer weed. This venue, we decided would prove our ultimate challenge.

When we began to fish we realised quickly that the Royalty would not yield its fish easily. We kept changing swims, but it seemed that no matter where we tried or what we did, small dace grabbed our breadflake bait before a bigger fish could be tempted. For some reason, I scaled down my tackle and changed to cheese for bait. This was cast into a pool which had formed behind a large rock in a fast, shallow run. Within a few minutes a great pull came, I struck, and my first-ever Avon barbel was 'on'. As the 2½lb bs hook-link did not allow much control, it took no less than 40 minutes to land that barbel. The then Head Bailiff, Brian Parkinson, weighed it at exactly 9lb.

Needless to say, after that, Bert and I returned to the

Royalty as often as possible. Even so, this was not too frequent an event, for it cost a whole week's spending money!

Two seasons later the Royalty produced my first-ever 5lb chub, but it was a further ten years before I slipped my net under my first chub over 6lb.

By this time I had met Bill Quinlan and, partly because Bert Dell had decided that ladies were marginally more interesting than big fish, Bill and I teamed up. Together we joined the Chiltern Specimen Group which subsequently merged with the Herts Specimen Group, eventually becoming known as the renowned Herts-Chiltern Anglers. Some of Britain's most successful and famous big-fish anglers of all time have been, or are, members. Jack Hilton is one.

Jack often used to join Bill and me during the winter months at, primarily, the Royalty, when carp fishing had 'finished'. My continued poor financial situation even meant that often Bill and Jack travelled down without me. It was on one such occasion that Jack caught a chub which stunned the big-fish fraternity – it weighed 7lb 2oz.

This truly monstrous river chub had been tempted from a small hole, carved out by the powerful winter currents, immediately upstream of a bridge's staunchion. Jack had fished this spot previously but the few small bites had failed to develop. To try to effect a cure, Jack used several pieces of crust as bait, each piece smaller than the one before. The smallest piece sat on the bend of the hook ending up with what he called a 'carrot-shaped crust'. To prove that the 7lb 2oz chub was no fluke, Jack caught the same fish again a few weeks later – a classic demonstration of big-fish angling. Jack was certainly one of our very best all-round big-fish anglers and, in my opinion, it is a pity he no longer fishes, having decided to 'call it a day' in 1976.

After Jack's captures we knew where a very big chub lived in a restricted area. I and many others thought that it would be easy to catch but, perhaps because he had been fooled twice before, the task proved very difficult to repeat.

Throughout the following winter, Bill and I tried, at some time or other, on our every visit, to catch Jack's big chub. All our attempts failed, until one Saturday in February the following year. I had been trying to think of something new and drawn a blank, so decided to return to square one and use bread – something we had avoided soon after Jack's second capture; surely, we reasoned, he wouldn't fall for a similar ploy a third time?

On the fateful day I tackled up in typical chub

● Fig 20 *Jack Hilton's 'carrot-shaped crust'*

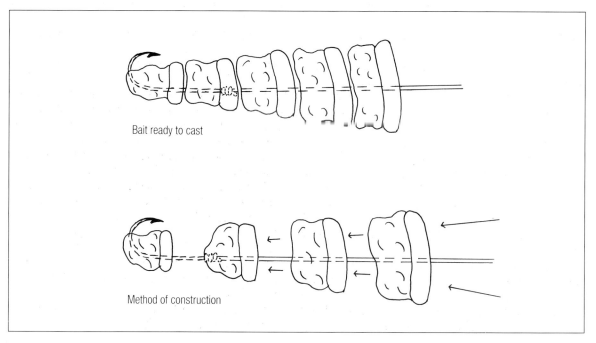

Bait ready to cast

Method of construction

fashion: 11ft fibre glass rod, with an all-through action; Mitchell reel loaded with 6lb bs monofil, to which was tied direct a pre-sharpened size 4 eyed hook; a single swan-shot link-leger and my favourite breadflake as bait completed the simple outfit.

I crept through shallow water to a dry hump, behind a curtain of foliage, just a few feet from the hole, and silently settled in. I was now sitting just a few feet from the swim, so close, in fact, that there was no need to cast. All I had to do was to hold the top of my rod over the hole and back-wind the reel until the bait, etc, was in position. The rod was then laid in two rod-rests, and I leant back to await events. Because the water in the hole was dead slack, I watched the line to detect any bite.

Twenty uneventful minutes dragged past, then the impossible happened – the bow in the line straightened and tightened. The answering strike met with a firm, yet living resistance. Immediately the chub was pulled away from any snags and out of the hole. Unfortunately, this was not the monster I was after, but a very tatty 4-pounder which was returned a hundred yards away.

Although I felt that I had messed up my chances, I lowered another piece of flake in the same spot, returned the rod to its rests and sat back expecting a very long wait. The day was pleasant enough – overcast and quite mild for the time of year – so I was happy to relax and drink tea. Only about a further thirty minutes passed when, to my great surprise, the line twitched before it steadily tightened. I struck and, as before, laid my rod over and heaved toward the main stream. He didn't come; instead, the rod top thumped around and almost all of the top joint was pulled under water. I gave everything the gear would take; on such a short line it was soon all over and I carried my prize well away from the water's edge.

With trembling hands, I spread the net away to display a magnificent chub, and there, on the gill cover, was the tell-tale black spots – without doubt it was Jack's chub. After removing the hook, the fish was suspended on my balance in a plastic carrier-bag. The result, I must confess, was a little disappointing – 6lb 8oz. Still, it was my first 6lb chub at last, and with ounces to spare.

I found Bill and his balance confirmed the weight; we took an ounce off for the bag to make the final weight 6lb 7oz. Bill shot a whole roll of film before my 6-pounder was lovingly returned. To my knowledge, it was never caught again, although we tried desperately.

Postscript

To me, the Royalty is the most interesting stretch of river and, when the winter's rains raise the water over its banks and into the fields, I love it. Many times I have stood up to my knees in water, a loaf of bread in my pocket for bait, catching and playing chub to my feet. Then I have been able to unhook them without them having to leave the water – for me, pure magic. Winter conditions seem to throw the chub off-balance and, consequently, they are apt to make a mistake. Let's hope this winter one of them will be my first 7-pounder.

A Smelly, Slimy, Horrible River Bream!
by Tony Arbery

It was 3.15am when I looked up from my lathe to check the time for the umpteenth time, wishing my last shift of the week would come rapidly to its end. At 4.30am, I was gone. Less than an hour later, after a quick stop at home to collect a freshly brewed flask of tea and a bait-box full of previously diced-up luncheon meat, I was once again in the car, on my way to collect Gordon Cross, my companion for a winter's day's fishing on the Dorset Stour.

The journey passed uneventfully, apart from the constant chat about what the day had in store for us. Our first stop was at one of my favourite haunts – The Little Chef, at Stony Cross – for breakfast. We left the restaurant not long after dawn and couldn't have wished for a better day for our purpose; it was mild, overcast, and with just a hint of rain carried on a balmy south-westerly breeze – in fact, perfect conditions.

In the fishery car park we soon donned our one-piece suits, waders, etc and, after tackling up, took the short walk through the trees down to the river's edge. We were pleased to note that water was almost bank high yet clear and had just the right tinge of greenish colour. As the thermometer was readied, I prayed for a water temperature of 43°F or over. My prayers were answered, for after a few minutes submersion, the instrument read 45°F. We agreed that these ideal conditions, both of the water and the weather, would give us a chance of the best of both worlds – chub during the day and barbel towards evening – heaven!

Our chosen method was quiver-tipped meat and, employing our usual roving tactics, we 'leap-frogged' past each other all down the west bank, trying every likely swim. It didn't take long for Gordon to score the first success – a 4lb 4oz chub in great condition. Soon after I emulated his success with a 4lb 7oz chub. And so it went on, though by the time we reached a favourite swim, Gordon was three chub to the good.

The new pitch was roomy enough for both of us to fish together. Sitting side-by-side, we cast simultaneously to the far edge of an extensive slack. Soon, as my bait stopped rolling, there came a savage pull. I am not sure whether I was over-exuberant or whether my tackle had been damaged in some way during an earlier tussle, but I struck, broke the line and fell off my chair. My fall, however, was broken by the biggest, freshest cow-pat imaginable! Gordon was reduced to helpless laughter and it was some time before he had recovered sufficiently to say, 'All you need now is to catch one of those smelly, slimy, horrible river bream and your day will be complete.' This remark started him laughing again and I don't know how he recovered his composure in time to hit his next bite.

This came before I had finished setting up again (with brand new 6lb Specimen Plus line) and was obviously the best fish of the day so far. After slipping the landing-net under it, I carried it well away from the river before weighing it. The result was 5lb 6oz of pristine chub to be entered in Gordon's notebook. The honours were duly done with the camera before the fish was carefully returned to the river. This was done well away from the swim, as we had reason to hope that there was still more to come and we didn't want to risk unnecessarily scaring any fish that remained in the successful area.

No sooner had my renewed tackle stopped rolling, on its first journey down the swim, when a savage bite almost pulled the rod from my hand. The answering strike was again followed by a resounding crack. It wasn't the line that broke this time, however. My almost new, very expensive, custom-built, carbon-fibre rod had disintegrated into dozens of pieces. I was left playing an obviously big fish on a cork handle with about 6in of shattered carbon sticking out of the end. As if to add insult to injury, as the fish was bullied impatiently to the waiting net, fragments of carbon rod popped to the surface and drifted downstream out of reach, so even the rod rings were unable to be salvaged. Then, finally, the hooked fish came into view – 'one of

those smelly, slimy, horrible river bream'. My disappointment hurt, as did the long walk back to the car to fetch my spare rod.

It was a good hour later when eventually I settled back down next to Gordon in the same swim. Good chap that he is, rather than take advantage of my predicament and empty the swim of fish, he had used the time I was away to have his lunch and thereby let any remaining fish recover from the previous happenings. Notwithstanding this fact, the fish proved unco-operative and the short winter's afternoon soon drifted by.

As evening approached, I suggested to Gordon that we try an area we had fished earlier, but to fish it from slightly lower downstream. Here, I had noticed, the water looked smoother than usual; perhaps the recent floods had scoured out a new hole. Gordon, however, elected to fish from his previous position.

My first cast in the new swim produced a bite so tentative that I couldn't visualise it afterwards, but from it a barbel was hooked – and it felt a big one at that. So it proved, and in the dying minutes of daylight Gordon slipped the net around 10lb 10oz of muscular dynamite. That, all things considered, evened the score between us; surely, Gordon's 5lb 6oz chub and my double-figure barbel were equally meritorious?

After photographing and carefully returning my prize, we fished on, in the same swims, for about a further hour with no more bites forthcoming. Now was the time to play our final, and trump, card.

We had pre-baited, several times earlier in the day, a wim in which we had enjoyed barbel successes in the past. This type of pre-baiting is a calculated gamble, of course – somebody else may move in and perhaps reap the rewards of your labour and forethought, especially if your comings and goings have been noticed – but, I think, a gamble well worth the risk. As far as we were aware, nobody had ventured anywhere near 'our swim' that day, and we very carefully and quietly moved in, for in this swim, we had previously learned, the barbel often fed right in the margins.

My first cast produced a 5½lb barbel – good, but not the stamp of fish we yearned for, though it encouraged Gordon to redouble his efforts. Twenty silent minutes later a good, old-fashioned, tremendous barbel bite almost pulled me out of my chair. There was no need to strike and another obviously big fish plunged at the end

● *Gordon Cross's 5lb 6oz chub from the Kennet*

Good Days

● *Tony Arbery with his 'double' barbel (10lb 3oz)*

of my line. During the ten-minute fight, the hooked barbel fought with stubborn power, but my tackle was sound and, eventually, he had to go in the waiting net. The pointer of the large Reuban Heaton dial balance again swung past the 10lb mark, stopping at 10lb 3oz.

Two 'doubles' on a winter's day is a very rare event indeed and had me almost jumping for joy; Gordon, on the other hand, now looked decidedly glum. When we returned to our seats, I could hear him muttering to himself about throwing me in the river if I caught another big barbel. As we both recast I jokingly said, 'Here comes number three'. Almost immediately another terrific bite heralded another hooked big barbel. Unfortunately (or, perhaps fortunately, as I didn't fancy

a cold bath at that time of night), after a lengthy fight the barbel got into a snag and the tackle was eventually recovered minus the hook.

At this juncture Gordon threw all his bait into the river and announced almost inaudibly through gritted teeth, 'if you want to fish any longer you will now have to give me some of *your* bait, as all mine is gone and I might as well pack up and go home if I can't use some of yours.' He was joking, of course; we were both using the same brand of luncheon meat (Sainsbury's). Some of my meat, however, had been cut up differently from his and it was this shape which had fooled the four barbel I had hooked that day. Rather than cutting the meat into cubes, I had cut it into slices ⅛in (3mm) thick, about 1½in (40mm) long by ½in (13mm) wide. This shape, I reckoned, would create more water resistance if put on the hook correctly. Therefore, it was more likely to

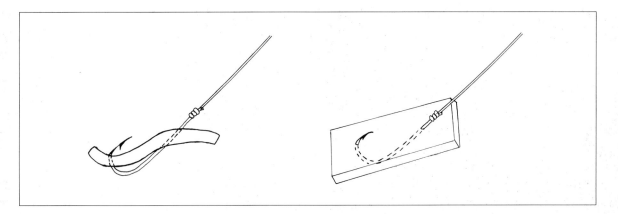

● Fig 21 *Method of hooking a slice of luncheon-meat*

flutter enticingly, emulating the carp boy's pop-up boilie rather than staying 'nailed' to the bottom. Other predicted advantages are: the new shape may just fool a particularly wily fish; the hook point can be left more exposed to encourage better hooking; and the weight of the hook may be neutralised.

Shortly after we had both recast, Gordon was into his first barbel of the day. It weighed a fraction over 8lb. Not long after, it was time to go home at the end of a great day's fishing. Gordon's result was four chub over 4lb – the best 5lb 6oz – and an 8lb barbel. I had three chub over 4lb, three barbel – including a brace of doubles – and a smelly, slimy, horrible river bream!

Postscript

I have been asked, after catching a 6lb-plus chub and a 14lb barbel, what are my ambitions for these species now. Well, although they are very difficult targets, whenever conditions appear suitable and coincide with my free time, then I will be out on the banks trying to beat them. This past winter, 1991–2, was no exception. My diary reminds me that fewer than a dozen trips were made to Dorset, partly because a serious illness kept me at home, and partly because it was one of the driest on record. Nevertheless, several barbel were captured, including two in double figures. The day before I took the second one was another red-letter occasion for me. The Dorset Stour was low and bright and its temperature a very promising 48°F; cloud cover was thin but low and there was only a whisper of wind. Obviously, these were excellent conditions for chub fishing, and so it proved. The *Angling Times* reported it thus:

Dad Shows He Knows Best!

Big fish specialist Len Arbery answered the leg-pulling from his son Tony in the best way he knew how – by smashing the pairs' chub records out of sight. After topping his dad's personal best with a magnificent 6lb 4oz specimen, young Tony's taunts were silenced when Len slid his net under a cracking 6lb 9oz Dorset Stour monster – one of the biggest chub reported this season.

Len was taking advantage of the spring-like weather by travelling to the Dorset Stour for a short afternoon/evening session in search of specimens. The Uxbridge, West London, toolroom foreman was using his usual roving style, link-legering any likely looking swim using meat bait. A far-bank slack produced the classic response to an upstream cast – a dropback bite, and the ensuing struggle indicated a barbel. But he was proved wrong when a massive chub broke the surface, and a career best dropped into the net – his third over the magical 6lb mark.

Len made the long journey back to the river the following day and made it a memorable double with a 10lb 14oz barbel. He said: 'Tony should have known better than to tempt providence by teasing me after his recent capture of our previous best chub. He made a similar mistake after capturing a family best 11lb 14oz barbel, a few weeks before I caught my 14-pounder that clinched for me that season's Drennan Cup.'

Appendix

Records

I am indebted to the National Federation of Anglers (NFA) and to the National Association of Specialist Anglers (NASA), for making the following notes available.

The British Record (rod-caught) Fish Committee

Aims and objectives

The committee exists to recognise and publish record weights of freshwater fish caught on rod and line, by fair angling methods, in the waters of England, Wales, Scotland and Northern Ireland.

To provide an adjudicating body to which freshwater anglers may submit claims for record fish taken by fair rod and line angling.

To investigate all such record claims to the fullest possible extent and maintain a permanent record of such investigations.

To establish and maintain accurately a list of British freshwater fish of record size and to publish this list frequently and make it readily available to all interested persons.

The activities of the committee are voluntary, and claims are considered and adjudicated upon, only on the basis that the committee shall be under no obligation whatsoever to claimants, that its decisions shall be final, and it shall not be obliged to give reasons for its decisions.

Halliday House 2 Wilson Street
Derby, DE1 1PG Tel: 0332 362000

How to claim a record fish

As soon as possible on capturing a potential record fish, contact any one of the committee members below:

Phil Smith (Warwickshire)	0203 687780
Neville Fickling (Lincolnshire)	0427 83731
Dr Bruno Broughton (Nottinghamshire)	0602 841703
Len Arbery (London)	0895 271009
Kevin Clifford (North Humberside)	0430 440624
Bryan Culley (Leicester)	0509 413797
Brian Crawford (Shropshire)	0952 591131

Rules

The Committee needs to be satisfied beyond all reasonable doubt that the fish was correctly identified and weighed, and was captured by the claimant by fair angling.

It reserves the right to accept, reject or delete any fish from its list without being compelled to give reasons for so doing.

The committee will use its discretion to examine claims, subject to the following requirements:

1. Photographs of the fish must be available which should be of good quality and preferably in colour. They should include shots of the angler holding the fish in a normal manner, and the fish lying on the ground next to an identifiable object.
2. The weighing scales and/or a Weights and Measures/Trading Standards Department certificate must be presented for inspection.
3. The weight must be verified by two independent witnesses who, for example, should not be relations of the claimant or a member of his club or party. NASA representatives are available as witnesses to verify a claim and can be contacted by phoning one of the committee.

Verification procedure

1 Upon catching a potential record fish, contact one of the committee.
2 This member will scrutinise the national list of representatives and contact by phone the person living nearest the place of capture. If he can't be contacted, the next nearest will be contacted.
3 He will attend as soon as possible, and should be aware of the rules regarding claims.
4 After his visit, during which we hope he will have verified the necessary details, you should then make a formal claim to the British Record (rod caught) Fish Committee via the NFA (Tel: 0332 362000).

How to weigh potential record fish

1 Wet weigh-sling/bag and squeeze out excess water.
2 Put weigh-sling/bag onto scales and zero to '0' as near as possible, but ensure the needle can still move and is not 'bottomed'. (Scales must be in a vertical position and held by the handle – not by the body.)
3 After zeroing, the scales should not be laid flat but must be kept in a vertical position.
4 The fish should be transferred to the weigh-sling/bag and suspended from the scales.
5 Have the reading on the scales witnessed in both cases (zeroing and weighing the fish).
6 Subtract the zeroed weight (if not actually at '0') from the total weight.
7 In the case of scales that have a pointer that rotates several times, you should repeat the weighing of the fish several times, counting the rotations carefully.

Submitting a formal record fish claim

(*Write out the following data*)

1 Fish species.
2 Weight in pounds and ounces (plus drams for small species). (Note scales used must be appropriate for size of species – do not use 32lb or 40lb scales for bleak or gudgeon, for example.)
3 Length (from tip of nose to fork of tail).
4 Maximum girth.
5 Location of water (*will be treated in confidence*).
6 Date and time of capture.
7 Description of bait and tackle used, including names of rod, reel, etc.
8 Name and address, postcode and phone number of claimant in block letters.
9 Any other relevant details.
10 For roach, rudd, chub, dace, silver bream, give numbers of scales in lateral line, plus count of rays in dorsal and anal fins. (*I would also advise including good quality close-up photographs showing relationship of dorsal and pelvic fins, head, etc. L.A.*)
11 Names, addresses, postcodes and telephone numbers of independent witnesses, plus their statements, if not witnessed by an official NASA representative.
12 Send application to NFA.

British Record Coarse Fish List (as at 29 January 1992)

Species Latin name		Weight				Date	Captor & Location
	lb	oz	dm	kg	g		
BARBEL *Barbus barbus*	14	6	0	6	520	1934	The Hon Aylmer Tryon Royalty Fishery, Hampshire Avon
BLEAK *Alburnas alburnas*	–	4	4	–	120	1982	B. Derrington River Monnow, Wye Mouth, Monmouthshire
BREAM (COMMON) *Abramis brama*	16	9	0	7	152	1991	M. McKeown Southern Water
BREAM (SILVER) *Abramis bjoerkna*	–	15	0	–	425	1988	D. E. Flack Grime Spring, Lakenheath, Suffolk
MILLER'S THUMB *Cottus gobio*	–	1	0	–	028	1983	R. Johnson Bramley & Shamley, Green River
CARP *Cyprinus carpio*	51	8	0	23	358	1980	C. Yates Redmire Pool, Hereford
CARP, CRUCIAN *Carassius carassius*	5	10	8	2	565	1976	G. Halls Lake Nr King's Lynn, Norfolk
CARP, GRASS *Ctenopharyngodon idella*	23	14	0	10	829	1991	G. Wallis Canterbury Lake
CATFISH (WELLS) *Siluris glanis*	43	8	0	19	730	1970	R. J. Bray Wilstone Reservoir, Tring, Hertfordshire
CHUB *Leuciscus cephalis*	8	4	0	3	743	1913	G. F. Smith Royalty Fishery, Hampshire, Avon
DACE *Leuciscus leuciscus*	1	4	4	–	574	1960	J. L. Gasson Little Ouse, Thetford, Norfolk
EEL *Anguilla anguilla*	11	2	0	5	046	1978	S. Terry Kingfisher Lake, Nr Ringwood, Hampshire
GUDGEON *Gobio gobio*	–	5	0	–	141	1990	D. H. Hull River Nadder, Salisbury, Wiltshire
MINNOW *Phoxinus phoxinus*	–	–	13	–	023	1981	R. Merrifield River Calder, Nelson, Lancashire
ORFE, GOLDEN *Leuciscus idus*	5	15	0	2	693	1990	G. Sherwin Lymmvale, Cheshire

Species		lb	oz	dr			Year	Angler / Location
PERCH	*Percia fluvatilis*	5	9	0	2	523	1985	J. Shayler, Furnace Lake, Kent
PIKE	*Esox lucius*	45	6	0	20	581	1990	G. O. Edwards, Llandeggfedd Reservoir, Pontypool, Gwent
WALLEYE	*Stizostedion vitreum*	11	12	0	5	329	1934	F. Adams, The Delph, Welney, Norfolk
ZANDER	*Stizostedion lucioperca*	18	8	0	8	390	1988	R. N. Meadows, Cambridge water
ROACH	*Rutilus rutilus*	4	3	0	1	899	1990	R. N. Clarke, Dorset Stour
RUDD	*Rutilus erythrophthalmus*	4	8	0	2	041	1933	Revd E. C. Alston, Thetford, Norfolk
RUFFE	*Gymnocephalus cernus*	–	5	4	–	148	1980	R. J. Jenkins, Cumbria
TENCH	*Tinca tinca*	14	3	0	6	435	1987	P. A. Gooriah, Wraysbury 1 Pit

Bibliography

Bibliographical Note

Besides providing extremely good reading, there are other perfectly valid reasons for the following Bibliography to contain some old and out-of-print titles. For far too many years I did not read old fishing books. For what, in the way of stimulus, I asked myself, could such works offer the modern progressive angler? The answer is much, as I shall explain.

Most big fish anglers will no doubt agree that the most significant development in bait presentation was the invention of the hair-rig. Understandably, most anglers consider this a relatively recent innovation, for it was Lennie Middleton and Kevin Maddocks, working in the late 1970s, who worked out the effectiveness of the hair-rig when fishing for carp. However, it is no less true that similar devices have been used by anglers of the past. In at least two well-loved, old fishing books, something similar to the hair-rig has been described. Here, within those dust-laden pages, they waited for someone to rediscover and exploit them. This may be difficult to believe, but perhaps you won't be so sceptical after perusing the following two passages (in both cases the italics in the excerpts are mine). The first is taken from Hugh Tempest Sheringham's *Coarse Fishing*, published in 1912.

> I believe water-snails, and fresh-water shrimps, and things like that, are the barbel's natural food. The trouble is putting them on a hook. Shrimps are tiny little things, and barbel hooks have to be pretty stout in the wire. Perhaps you could use some sticky stuff like seccotine, and simply stick four or five shrimps to the hook. Snails might be *tied on with fine thread.* Frenchmen use aniseed cake for many kinds of fish, and they *tie it to their hooks with thread.* They call it 'La Noquette' we don't know everything about fishing in England, though we think we do.

If it seems that eighty years is a long time for the hair-rig to have been in existence, the following extract is even more interesting: 'Some have directed to cut the cheese into thin pieces, and toast it, and then *tie it on the hook with fine silk.*' Believe it or not, this quotation is taken from a 1907 facsimile reprint of the first edition of Izaac Walton's *The Compleat Angler*, published no less than 340 years ago, in 1653. Surely, as this is one of the most widely read books in the English language, at some time during the course of the past three and a half centuries, someone must have read these words and benefited from them. My only regret is that their experiences are not recorded.

These passages are not intended to detract from the work of Lennie and Kevin, because I, as much as anyone else, have much to thank them both for.

Aflalo, F. G., *Fishermen's Weather* (A & C Black, 1906)

Arbery, Len, *Catching Big Tench* (David & Charles, 1989)

Bailey, John, *The Great Anglers* (David & Charles, 1990)

— . — . , *Roach: The Gentle Giants* (Crowood, 1987)

Bailey, John, and Martyn Page, *Pike: The Predator Becomes the Prey* (Crowood, 1985)

Barnes, Tag, *The Exploring Angler* (Eyre & Spottiswoode, 1945)

'BB' (Denys Watkins-Pitchford), *The Fisherman's Bedside Book* (Eyre & Spottiswoode, 1945)

Bickerdyke, J. (C. H. Cook), *The Book of the All-Round Angler* (The Bazaar, Exchange and Mart, 1912)

Buckland, Frank, *The Natural History of British Fishes* (Society for Promoting Christian Knowledge, 1883)

Buller, Fred, *Pike* (Macdonald, 1971)

Chalmers, Patrick, *At the Tail of the Weir* (Philip Allan, 1932)

Cholmondely-Pennell, H., *The Book of the Pike* (Routledge, 1865)

– . – ., *The Modern Practical Angler* (Routledge, 1870)

'Faddist' (Edward Ensom), *Memorable Coarse Fish* (Burlington, 1953)

– . – ., *Roach and Dace Fishing* (Seeley, 1953)

Falkus, Hugh and Fred Buller, *Freshwater Fishing* (Macdonald & Janes, 1975)

Fickling, Neville, *Pike Fishing in the Eighties* (Beekay, 1982)

Forbes, David Carl, *Successful Roach Fishing* (David & Charles, 1973).

– . – ., *Small Stream Fishing* (George Newnes, 1966)

Foster, David, *The Scientific Angler* (Bemrose and Sons, 5th ed 1893)

Foster, Fred, *Swing Tipping* (Cassell, 1976)

Geen, Philip, *Days Stolen for Sport* (T. Werner Laurie, 1907)

Gibbinson, Jim, *Modern Specimen Hunting* (Beekay, 1983)

Guttfield, Frank, *In Search of Big Fish* (EMAP, 1964)

Guttfield, Frank, (ed), *The Big Fish Scene* (Ernest Benn, 1978)

Head, Len, *River Fishing* (Crowood, 1985)

Howes, William J., *The Quest for Barbel* (Thorsons, 1960)

– . – ., *The Sporting Chub* (Thorsons, 1960)

Ingham, Maurice and Richard Walker, *Drop Me A Line* (MacGibbon & Kee, 1953)

Marsden, Graham, *Advanced Coarse Fishing* (A & C Black, 1980)

Marshall-Hardy, Eric, *Angling Ways* (Herbert Jenkins, 4th ed, 1956)

Martin, J. W., *The Nottingham Style of Float Fishing and Spinning* (Sampson Low, Marston, Searle & Elvington, 1882)

– . – ., *Coarse Fish Angling* (Brendon & Son, 1908)

– . – ., *Barbel and Chub Fishing* (*The Angler*, 1896)

– . – ., *My Fishing Days and Fishing Ways* (J. Brendon & Son, 1906)

– . – ., *Roach, Rudd & Bream Fishing in Many Waters* (Albert Frost & Sons, 2nd ed, 1905)

– . – ., *Days Among the Pike and Perch* (Jonathon Cape, 1907)

Norman, John, *Coarse Fishing with the Experts* (Allen & Unwin, 1956)

Parker, Capt L. A., *This Fishing: or Angling Arts and Artifices* (Cleaver-Hume, 2nd ed, 1960)

Pye, Dennis, *The Way I Fish* (EMAP, 1963)

Rickards, Barry, *Angling: Fundamental Principles* (Boydell, 1986)

Seaman, Kenneth, *The Complete Chub Angler* (David & Charles, 1976)

Sheringham, H., *Coarse Fishing* (A & C Black, 1912)

. . ., *An Open Creel* (Methuen, 1910)

– . – ., *An Angler's Hours* (Macmillan, 1905)

'Silver Doctor' (Lewis Smith), *Angling From Many Angles* (Mrs E. G. Lewis-Smith, 1946)

Smith, Phil, *Rainbow's End* (Ironbridge Publications, 1987)

Sosin, Mark and John Clark, *Through the Fish's Eye* (André Deutsch, 1976)

Stone, Peter, *Big Chub* (Beekay, 1983)

– . – ., *Bream and Barbel* (EMAP, 1963)

Taylor, Fred J., *Angling in Earnest* (MacGibbon & Kee, 1962)

– . – ., *Favourite Swims* (MacGibbon & Kee, 1961)

– . – ., *My Fishing Years* (David & Charles, 1981)

Travis-Jenkins, J., *The Fishes of the British Isles* (Frederick Warne, 2nd ed, 1958)

Vaughan, Bruce (ed), *Top Ten* (Beekay, 1983)

Walker, Richard, *Still Water Angling* (MacGibbon & Kee, 1953)

– . – ., *Walker's Pitch* (Allen & Unwin, 1959)

Webb, Ray and Barry Rickards, *Fishing for Big Pike* (A & C Black, 2nd ed, 1976)

Wheat, Peter, *The Fighting Barbel* (Ernest Benn, 1967)

– . – ., *Pelham Manual of River Coarse Fishing* (Pelham, rev ed, 1978)

West, Trefor and Tony Miles, *Quest for Barbel* (Crowood, 1991)

Yates, Chris, *The Deepening Pool* (Unwin Hyman, 1990)

Useful Addresses

Associations

Anglers' Co-operative Association (ACA), 23 Castlegate, Grantham, Lincolnshire NG31 6SW

Barbel Catchers' Club, c/o Alan Slater, 129 Elgar Road, Reading, Berkshire

Carp Society, 33 Covert Road, Hainault, Ilford, Essex IG6 3AZ

National Association of Specialist Anglers (NASA), c/o Dr Kathy Fickling, 'Kilgarth', 27 Lodge Lane, Upton, Gainsborough, Lincolnshire

Pike Anglers' Club (PAC), Chris Leibbrandt, 23 Theocs Close, Tewkesbury Park, Tewkesbury, Gloucestershire GL20 5TX

Record Fish Claims

See Appendix, p157–9.

Specialist Tackle Shops

Addlestone Angling Centre (Pete Collins), 166 Station Road, Addlestone, Surrey KT15 2BA

Bournemouth Fishing Lodge (Ivor Brittain), 904 Wimborne Road, Moordown, Bournemouth

Davis Angling (Graham Pepler), 75 Bargates, Christchurch, Dorset BH23 1QE

Kennet Tackle, 3 The Birdwood Centre, Station Road, Thatcham, Berkshire RG13 4YA

Middlesex Angling Centre (Keith Sellick), 1288 Greenford Road, Greenford, Middlesex UB6 0HH.

Pro Fishing Tackle (Tony Croft), 258 Barrack Road, Christchurch, Dorset

Reading Angling Centre, 69 Northumberland Avenue, Reading, Berkshire

Ringwood Tackle (Ted Waterman), 5 The Bridges, Ringwood, Hampshire

Angling Permits

Christchurch Angling Club, c/o P. Reading, 17 Mayford Road, Branksome, Dorset BH12 1PT

Leisure Sport Angling Club, Thorpe Park, Staines Lane, Chertsey, Surrey KT16 8PN

Reading & District Angling Association, c/o Reading Angling Centre, 69 Northumberland Avenue, Reading, Berkshire

Ringwood & District Angling Association, c/o J. Levell, 4 Forestside Gardens, Poulner, Ringwood, Hampshire

Royalty Fishery, The Bailiff's House, off Bargates, Christchurch, Dorset

Throop Fisheries, Glenn Sutcliffe. South Lodge, Holdenhurst Village, Bournemouth BH8 0EF

Rod Licences

National Rivers Authority (NRA), 30–4 Albert Embankment, London SE1 7TL

Note

The National Rivers Authority announced that a single national rod licence covering all species of fish would come into effect in England and Wales from 1 January 1992. This replaces the old system of over 100 rod licences in different parts of the country, which is 'divisive and expensive to operate', and remove the need for anglers to have separate licences to fish either for salmon and sea trout, or for all other species. The new licence costs £12.50 and allows anglers to fish with two rods throughout England and Wales, where rules and byelaws permit, at no extra charge. Young anglers aged from 12 to 16, the disabled, and OAPs (aged 60 and over), will only have to pay £6.50.

Anyone who fishes in fresh water must have an NRA licence; these are available from any good tackle shop, etc.

Bait Suppliers

Streamselect Ltd, Manufacturers of Richworth Products (ie, frozen boilies, Shelf-life boilies, blast-frozen dead-baits, etc). Island Farm Avenue, West Molesey, Surrey KT8 0UZ

Specialist Tackle Manufacturers

Len Arbery (hand-built landing-nets and reels, antique reel repairs and renovation), 179 Park Road, Uxbridge, Middlesex UB8 1NP

Drennan International Ltd, Leopold Works, Leopold Street, Oxford

Edward Barder (Hand-made rods and tackle), The New Barn, North End, Nr Newbury, Berkshire RG15 0AY

Fox International, Fowler Road, Hainault Industrial Estate, Hainault, Essex IG6 3UT

Gardener Tackle, 2 Pepper Box Lane, Palmers Cross, Bramley, Surrey

John Roberts Developments, 102 Minster Road, Westgate-on-Sea, Kent CT8 8DG

Shimano Reels, Unit B2 Lakeside, Phoenix Way, Enterprise Park, Llansamlet, Swansea SA7 9EH

Swallow Centre-pin Reel (Dave Swallow), Bridge Farm, Iford Bridge, Nr Ringwood, Hampshire

Index